1st Workshop Towards Ethical and Inclusive Conversational AI: Language Attitudes, Linguistic Diversity, and Language Rights (TEICAI 2024)

St. Julian's, Malta
22 March 2024

ISBN: 978-1-7138-9462-9

Printed from e-media with permission by:

Curran Associates, Inc.
57 Morehouse Lane
Red Hook, NY 12571

Some format issues inherent in the e-media version may also appear in this print version.

Printed with permission by Curran Associates, Inc. (2025)

Association for Computational Linguistics
209 N. Eighth Street
Stroudsburg, Pennsylvania 18360

Phone: 1-570-476-8006
Fax: 1-570-476-0860

acl@aclweb.org

Additional copies of this publication are available from:

Curran Associates, Inc.
57 Morehouse Lane
Red Hook, NY 12571 USA
Phone: 845-758-0400
Fax: 845-758-2633
Email: curran@proceedings.com
Web: www.proceedings.com

TEICAI 2024

The 1st Workshop Towards Ethical and Inclusive Conversational AI: Language Attitudes, Linguistic Diversity, and Language Rights

Proceedings of the Workshop

March 22, 2024

The TEICAI organisers and presenters gratefully acknowledge the support from the EU COST Action CA19102 "Language in the Human-Machine Era".

Supported by

LANGUAGE IN THE HUMAN-MACHINE ERA

Association for Computational Linguistics (ACL)
209 N. Eighth Street
Stroudsburg, PA 18360
USA
Tel: +1-570-476-8006
Fax: +1-570-476-0860
acl@aclweb.org

Introduction

Welcome to the 1st workshop Towards Ethical and Inclusive Conversational AI: Language Attitudes, Linguistic Diversity, and Language Rights, co-located with EACL 2024!

Our work on the intersection of language ideologies, language rights, and conversational AI started in 2021 within EU COST Action "Language in the Human-Machine Era"(LITHME). Researchers working on the crossroads of these topics contributed to three editions of international LITHME conferences in 2021-2023, and more focused work on language ideologies and conversational AI has been performed during the CONVERSATIONS 2022 workshop. Finally, we decided to give it the shape of a workshop at EACL 2024 in order to reach a broader academic audience and intensify the exchange within the language technology community.

While we have seen a rapid increase and diversification of language-based technologies over the last two decades, their development is still very much driven by technology designers and technologically relevant concerns. Users' needs and their communicative affordances have played a minor role and are often only addressed when commercial interests are at risk. For example, the dialogue patterns of conversational AI tend to lack adaptability to different user groups and their sociocultural contexts. Overall, technologies are based on structural notions of language and are still not able to do justice to the complexity of human communication.

In addition, the human rights regulation of AI-based conversational technology is scarce in many areas. When it comes to language rights, striking a balance between technological advancement and ensuring that conversational technology contributes positively to linguistic diversity and inclusion is essential. Addressing this requires a holistic approach that involves dialogue and collaboration among technologists, linguists, policymakers, and communities affected by conversational AI systems.

In addition, training data used to build conversational AI of the newest generation is mostly conceptually and medially written language. Furthermore, existing methods prioritize the formal and mechanized aspects of language, neglecting the gestural, social, and emotional elements that are fundamental to communication. Signed languages, due to their inherently multimodal nature and spatial-contextual dependencies are still excluded from the conversational AI space.

While the socio-linguistic community is intensively discussing the issues mentioned above, these topics have not yet completely arrived in the Computational Linguistics and NLP community. The goal of the workshop is to bring together researchers from all communities and intensify the academic exchange in order to cultivate a multidisciplinary approach to the development of conversational AI that can better serve diverse global audiences.

The program of TEICAI 2024 includes two keynote talks, seven paper presentations and one round-table discussion.

The organizing committee would like to express its appreciation to the authors who submitted papers, the reviewers, the panelists, and the invited speakers for their invaluable contributions. We are already looking forward to the workshop's next edition!

Best wishes,
The TEICAI organizing committee

Organizing Committee

Organizing Committee Members

Sviatlana Höhn, LuxAI, Luxembourg
Nina Hosseini-Kivanani, University of Luxembourg, Luxembourg
Dimitra Anastasiou, Luxembourg Institute of Science and Technology, Luxembourg
Bettina Migge, University College Dublin, Ireland
Angela Soltan, State University of Moldova, Moldova
Doris Dippold, University of Surrey, UK
Ekaterina Kamlovskaya, Luxembourg National Data Service, Luxembourg
Fred Philippy, Zortify, Luxembourg

Program Committee

Program Committee

Dimitra Anastasiou, Luxembourg Institute of Science and Technology, Luxembourg
Matt Coler, University of Groningen, Netherlands
Jelske Dijkstra, Fryske Akademy / Mercator Research Centre, Netherlands
Doris Dippold, University of Surrey, UK
Siwen Guo, Zortify, Luxembourg
Leopold Hillah, University of Luxembourg, Luxembourg
Sviatlana Höhn, LuxAI, Luxembourg
Raquel Lázaro Gutiérrez, University of Alcalá, Spain
Daniel Leix Palumbo, University of Groningen, Netherlands
Bettina Migge, University College Dublin, Ireland
Javier Moreno-Rivero, City University of New York, USA
Aria Nourbakhsh, University of Luxembourg, Luxembourg
Fred Philippy, Zortify, Luxembourg
Angela Soltan, State University of Moldova, Moldova

Invited Speakers

Justine Cassell, INRIA Paris, France
Chakravarthi Bharathi Raja, University of Galway, Ireland

Keynote Talk: Culturally-Aware Educational Language Technologies

Justine Cassell
INRIA Paris, France
2024-03-22 09:30:00 – Room: **Bastion 1**

Abstract: Children seamlessly shift their ways of speaking, adopting and adapting language they hear spoken by adults around them, as well as constructing their own variants. These speaking styles play an important role as children experiment with who they want to be, and how they want to be perceived. They also allow children growing up in situations where different dialects or languages are in contact to mark their affiliation to dominant and minority ethnic, racial, and gender identities. Young people who move between marginalized and mainstream communities often report code-switching as a way to maintain affiliation with their home community, while also making their way in a world where the standard dialect is associated with various kinds of success. However, moving back and forth may lead to what Ogbu (2008) has called "oppositional culture" to describe how school systems may inadvertently set up a situation where the student feels the need to define her identity contra the expectations of the school, and for that reason to refuse the dialect that the school insists on. Unfortunately, language technologies, including and very persistently, educational technologies, may inadvertently carry negative stereotypes about ethnicity and how it is carried in language, leading to stress and lack of a sense of agency as children try to navigate a path that allows them to benefit both from the support of their community and the opportunities offered by mainstream education. My students and I have examined this issue by building "culturally-aware" educational language technologies, and specifically "virtual peers" that either speak only the child's own dialect, or that model a code-switching strategy between what linguists call low-prestige and high-prestige dialects. Results using a variety of methodological approaches, in both one-shot and longitudinal studies, demonstrate the positive impact of technology such as these that take issues of culture, and of power, into account on children's school performance. On the other hand, careful assessments of the children's reactions to the technologies shows that they will need further development to improve the children's own internalized biases against low-prestige dialect speakers.

Keynote Talk: Language Technology for Equality, Diversity and Inclusion

Bharathi Raja Chakravarthi
University of Galway, Ireland
2024-03-22 14:40:00 – Room: **Bastion 1**

Abstract: Equality, Diversity and Inclusion (EDI) is an important agenda across every field throughout the world. Language as a major part of communication should be inclusive and treat everyone with equality. Today's large internet community uses language technology (LT) and has a direct impact on people across the globe. EDI is crucial to ensure everyone is valued and included, so it is necessary to build LT that serves this purpose. Recent results have shown that big data and deep learning are entrenching existing biases and that some algorithms are even naturally biased due to problems such as 'regression to the mode'. Our focus is on creating LT that will be more inclusive of gender, racial, sexual orientation, persons with disability. Over the past few years, systems have been developed to control online content and eliminate abusive, offensive or hate speech content. However, people in power sometimes misuse this form of censorship to obstruct the democratic right of freedom of speech. Therefore, it is imperative that research should take a positive reinforcement approach towards online content that is encouraging, positive and supportive. Until now, most studies have focused on solving this problem of negativity in the English language, though the problem is much more than just harmful content. Furthermore, it is multilingual as well.

Roundtable: The magic components of success: multidisciplinary collaboration among language rights, language ideology and conversational AI communities.

2024-03-22 16:00:00 – Room: **Bastion 1**

Abstract: Discussions about difficulties and key success factors in multidisciplinary projects have been ongoing since multidisciplinary collaborations exist, and the problems mentioned in those discussions frequently echo each other and include problems with communication, differences in terminology, theories and research methods, different approaches to knowledge creation and different community cultures. While these issues are still valid in the TEICAI community, we would like to look into more specific issues related to the specific communes of language ideologies, language rights and conversational AI, and structural issues related to research organisation, funding and academic culture in general.
In the round table, we want to highlight personal perspectives of researchers involved in multidisciplinary collaborations on the intersection of conversational AI, language ideologies and language rights. We want to listen to perspectives of researchers in different career stages:

- working mainly on technology and collaborate with researchers in language ideologies and/or language rights;
- working mainly in language rights and/or language ideologies and collaborating with researchers working mainly on technology aspects of conversational AI.

Further, we want to zoom out and understand how these personal experiences are embedded in a bigger picture of academic research.
Following the end of the roundtable, we will be dedicated to translating these discussions into a tangible set of recommendations aimed at fostering an ethical and inclusive future for conversational AI. These guidelines will be published across a variety of channels, aiming to inspire and provide direction to both the existing and next generations of field practitioners.

Panellists

- Nina Hosseini-Kivanani (PhD student, University of Luxembourg, LU)
- Doris Dippold (Senior Lecturer, University of Surrey, UK)
- Valentina Pyatkin (Postdoctoral Researcher, Allen Institute for AI, USA)
- Justine Cassel (Professor, INRIA Paris, FR and CMU, USA)

Moderator: Sviatlana Höhn (Postdoctoral researcher, LuxAI, LU)

Table of Contents

Program

Friday, March 22, 2024

09:00 - 09:30 *Welcome and Introduction*

09:30 - 10:30 *Keynote Talk by Justine Cassel: "Culturally-Aware Educational Language Technologies"*

10:30 - 11:00 *Coffee Break*

11:00 - 12:00 *Paper Session 1*

Why academia should cut back general enthusiasm about CAs
Alessia Giulimondi

Socio-cultural adapted chatbots: Harnessing Knowledge Graphs and Large Language Models for enhanced context awarenes
Jader Camboim de Sá, Dimitra Anastasiou, Marcos Da Silveira and Cédric Pruski

Bridging the Language Gap: Integrating Language Variations into Conversational AI Agents for Enhanced User Engagement
Marcellus Amadeus, Jose Roberto Homeli da Silva and Joao Victor Pessoa Rocha

Non-Referential Functions of Language in Social Agents: The Case of Social Proximity
Sviatlana Höhn

12:00 - 13:45 *Lunch Break*

13:45 - 14:40 *Paper Session 2*

How Do Conversational Agents in Healthcare Impact on Patient Agency?
Kerstin Denecke

How should Conversational Agent systems respond to sexual harassment?
Laura De Grazia, Alex Peiró Lilja, Mireia Farrús Cabeceran and Mariona Taulé

Making a Long Story Short in Conversation Modeling
Yufei Tao, Tiernan Mines and Ameeta Agrawal

Friday, March 22, 2024 (continued)

14:40 - 15:30	*Keynote Talk by Bharathi Raja Chakravarthi: "Language Technology for Equality, Diversity and Inclusion"*
15:30 - 16:00	*Coffee Break*
16:00 - 16:40	*Round-Table: "The magic components of success: multidisciplinary collaboration among language rights, langauge ideology and conversational AI communities"*
16:40 - 16:50	*Closing Words*

How Do Conversational Agents in Healthcare Impact on Patient Agency?

Kerstin Denecke
Bern University of Applied Sciences
Quellgasse 21, 2502 Biel/Bienne
Switzerland
kerstin.denecke@bfh.ch

Abstract

In healthcare, agency refers to the ability of patients to actively participate in and control their health through collaborating with providers, informed decision-making and understanding health information. Conversational agents (CAs) are increasingly used for realizing digital health interventions, but it is still unclear how they are enhancing patient agency. This paper explores which technological components are required to enable CAs impacting on patient agency, and identifies metrics for measuring and evaluating this impact. We do this by drawing on existing work related to developing and evaluating healthcare CAs and through analysis of a concrete example of a CA. As a result, we identify five main areas where CAs enhance patient agency, namely by: improved access to health information, personalized advice, increased engagement, emotional support and reduced barriers to care. For each of these areas, specific technological functions have to be integrated into CAs such as sentiment and emotion analysis methods that allow a CA to support emotionally.

1 Introduction

In recent years, conversational agents (CAs) have gained significant attention in the healthcare industry for their potential to revolutionize patient care and empower individuals to take control of their health (Bates, 2019). These computer-based systems use artificial intelligence (AI) and natural language processing (NLP) to simulate human-like conversations and provide personalized support and information to patients. They can answer questions, provide medical information, remind patients of medication schedules (Tschanz et al., 2018), and even provide mental health support (Denecke et al., 2020b), all in a conversational format. This interaction model is particularly significant because it closely aligns with the natural human tendency to talk, making these tools both intuitive and effective for a wide range of patients. However, there is a need to explore by which technological components CAs are enabled to impact on patient agency and how this impact could be measured and evaluated. Incorporating this knowledge into the development of healthcare CA would help to ensure that patient agency can be positively impacted by the use of these systems.

Patient agency has been defined in different ways. Street et al. consider patient agency in the context of communication between patient and healthcare professional and define it as self-efficacy and empowerment (Street Jr et al., 2009). In contrast, O'Hair et al. rather consider the participatory aspect of patient agency and claim that "patient agency requires skills across the spectrum of participation in care, ranging from active participation in medical encounters and decision-making to self-care skills for managing everyday health-related activities" (O'Hair et al., 2003). Another perspective on agency is related to health literacy and the language of health information and patient-doctor interaction (Hunter et al., 2015).

By agency in healthcare we refer in this paper to the ability and empowerment of patients to actively participate, make informed decisions and exercise control over their health and healthcare. It includes the ability to access, understand and use health information, to engage in a collaborative decision-making process with healthcare providers, and to take proactive steps to manage their health and well-being (Bok et al., 2022). The importance of this issue is underscored by the evolving role of patients in their healthcare journey (Joseph et al., 2020).

This definition emphasizes the multifaceted nature of agency, highlighting not only the decision-making and self-management aspects, but also the critical role of understanding and engaging with health information, which is particularly relevant in

Proceedings of the 1st Worskhop on Towards Ethical and Inclusive Conversational AI: Language Attitudes, Linguistic Diversity, and Language Rights (TEICAI 2024) , pages 1–8
March 22, 2024

the era of digital health solutions realized as CAs. Therefore, in the context of health CAs, agency refers to the extent to which these digital tools enhance or facilitate patient empowerment and involvement in their healthcare.

It is important to consider the agency of CAs in healthcare separately from traditional apps, as the interactive nature of conversations can make the experience more engaging and less passive. Navigation and interaction are very different. Many CAs are built with Artificial Intelligence and learn or adapt based on user interactions, allowing for more tailored and relevant responses over time, unlike static health apps. CAs can provide immediate feedback and answers to health-related questions, which is not always the case with other health apps that may require navigation through different sections to obtain information. CAs, especially those with well-designed personalities, can create a sense of connection and trust that is harder to achieve with standard health apps. They can handle more complex interactions, such as follow-up questions or clarifications, providing a deeper and more satisfying user experience. Advanced CAs can understand and respond to context, providing more relevant and personalized advice than traditional apps.

In previous work, we introduced a framework supposed to support evaluation and development of health CAs (Denecke, 2023). It comprises concrete metrics for evaluation, heuristics but also checklists that can be used during the CA development to ensure quality of the developed system. The aim of the current paper is to extend the framework by metrics to ensure that a health CA positively impacts on the patient agency. For this purpose, we will first answer the question on how a health CA can impact on patient agency. Then, we will assess how the existing framework covers the aspects of agency identified. Finally, we will collect metrics and checklists to be added to the framework to cover the facets of agency and measure agency.

2 Methods

In this paper, we answer the following research questions (RQ):

- RQ1: How do CAs impact on patient agency?
- RQ2: Which technology is needed to achieve the impact on agency?
- RQ3: How to evaluate the impact of the technology on agency?

To answer our research questions, we first identify aspects how CAs contribute to patients' agency. This will be done based on existing work related to the development and analysis of CAs in healthcare (Denecke et al., 2019; Gashi et al., 2021) and by reviewing literature on health CAs. Secondly, we collect the technological requirements that a CA must fulfill in order to ensure that the effects identified in the first step can be achieved, i.e. that a specific health CA can have an impact on the agency. This is done by analyzing an example of a health CA and mapping of the agency aspects from step 1 to technologies that are used to contribute to agency. In a third step, we evaluation categories ans metrics to allow researchers and developers to evaluate the impact of their CA on patient agency. Figure 1 summarizes the method and its results.

Hypothesizing that CAs implement specific technologies and functionalities to achieve an impact on the patient agency, an evaluation requires first to assess whether the technology needed to achieve an impact on agency is available in a CA with a required quality. Therefore, we map the development and evaluation framework proposed by Denecke et al. to the aspects of agency that have been identified in the first step (Denecke, 2023). The framework considers nine aspects from a general perspective (accessibility, ease of use, engagement, classifier performance, flexibility, content accuracy, context awareness, error tolerance, security), five aspects from a response generation perspective (appropriateness of responses, comprehensibility, speed of responses, empathy, linguistic accuracy), one aspect from a response understanding perspective (understanding), and three aspects from an aesthetics perspective (background color and content, font type and size, button color, shape, icon) (Denecke, 2023). It makes suggestions for tools and heuristics to evaluate these aspects. The framework comprises aspects to be considered not only as part of a system evaluation, but already during the development. We will identify missing aspects to measure and ensure the impact on agency and come up with suggestions for additional metrics based on available literature for extending the framework.

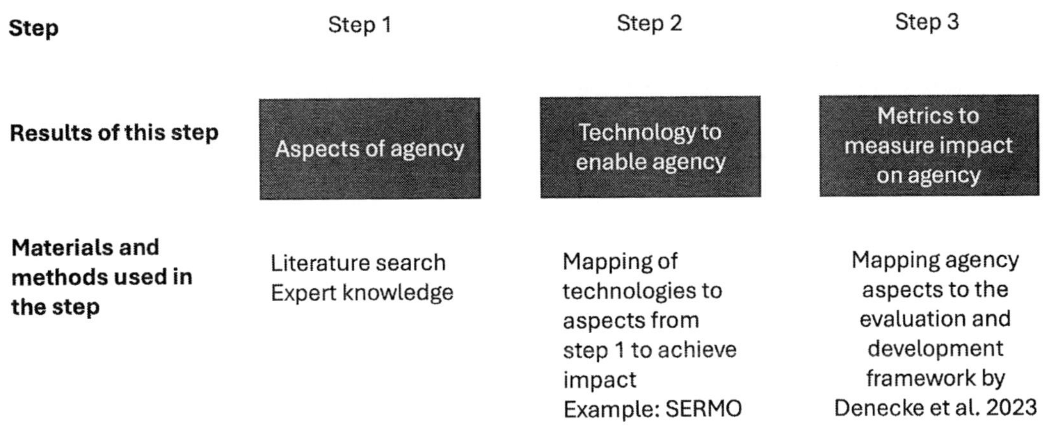

Figure 1: Method to answer our research questions comprising 3 steps

3 Impact of Conversational Agents in Healthcare on Patients' Agency

CAs applied in healthcare contexts, i.e. to deliver health interventions, can impact on patients' agency in several ways. These characteristics (C) of the impact are listed in the following and shown in figure 2.

C1: Improved access to health information and health literacy: Through dialogue, CAs can help improve a patient's understanding of their health condition and treatment options (May and Denecke, 2020). They can be accessible 24/7, providing patients with immediate answers to their questions. They can even guide patients through the decision-making process, providing tailored information to help them weigh up the pros and cons of different treatment options. This constant availability can help reduce the knowledge gap and increase the patient's ability to self-manage health issues in real time.

C2: Personalization and tailored advice: CAs can adapt their responses based on patient input, providing a more personalized healthcare experience. This can empower patients to make informed decisions tailored to their specific needs and circumstances. Even more advanced CAs can provide personalized health advice based on the patient's health records and current health state, which can be more effective than generic information (Kocaballi et al., 2019).

C3: Improved patient engagement: CAs can engage patients more actively in their healthcare journey (Denecke et al., 2020a). They can monitor patient symptoms and provide feedback or reminders, which can help patients understand the implications of their health behaviors (Larbi et al., 2022). By fostering a two-way interaction, CAs can help patients feel more involved and in control of their health decisions. Engaged patients are more likely to be proactive in their care (Barello et al., 2012), which is a critical aspect of agency.

C4: Emotional support and trust: CAs can provide emotional support to a patient, creating a sense of trust and comfort (Meng and Dai, 2021). This can encourage patients to express their concerns more openly, leading to better care and treatment compliance. When offering psychological support, CAs can help patients cope with the emotional aspects of their health conditions, which can be empowering and improve their overall wellbeing (Denecke et al., 2020b).

C5: Reducing healthcare barriers: For patients with disabilities or those who are less tech-savvy, a CA can be more accessible and easier to use than traditional apps. For individuals in remote areas, those with mobility problems or those who fear stigmatisation, CAs can reduce barriers to accessing health services and advice, thereby increasing the ability of these patients to seek and receive care (Nadarzynski et al., 2021).

4 Example: Emotion regulation with SERMO

In this section, we consider a concrete example of a CA and analyze which functionalities it includes to achieve the various aspects of patient agency.

SERMO is a health CA for regulating emotions and dealing with thoughts and feelings (Denecke et al., 2020b). It implements elements for cognitive

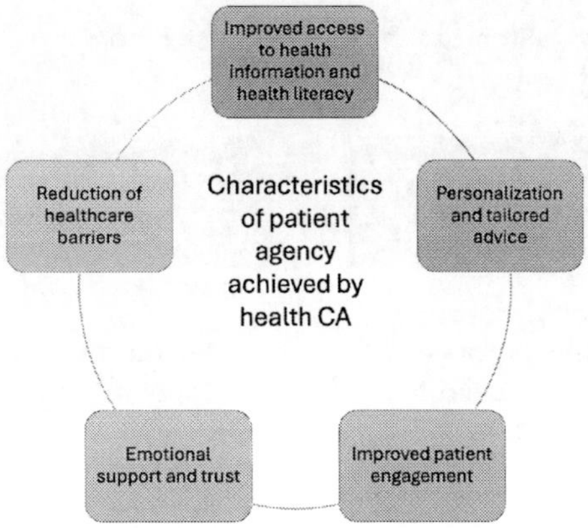

Figure 2: 5 aspects of how CA impact on patients' agency

behavior therapy. Specifically, it asks the user on a daily basis on events that happened and emotions caused by these events. Depending on the emotion, appropriate suggestions are made to the user. SERMO improves access to health information and in this way the user's health literacy (C1). It provides information on the system and its capabilities, but more importantly on cognitive behavior therapy which is the underlying clinical model and explains emotions. Also information on counseling services is provided, however, not by the chat function but by the app in which the CA is integrated.

SERMO is actively collecting information on events and emotions from the user natural language input and analyses them using Natural Language Processing (NLP) techniques and emotion analysis methods. Based on this information, tailored advice is given (C2). Only information explicitly entered by the user is used for this personalization of advice.

Using the mood diary, users can keep track of their emotions and how they handled them. SERMO helps in setting goals and in monitoring the emotions over time. In this way, it supports in understanding their behavior and how to deal with it (C3). The collected information can be discussed with a therapist which contributes to active decision-making and engagement.

A core element of SERMO is the recognition and classification of emotions and provision of appropriate advises. This is realized using NLP and emotion analysis methods. In this way, SERMO provides emotional support (C4). It could be used 24/7 without the need of a therapist or physician, thus helps in reducing healthcare barriers (C5) - however, it has not yet been assessed how SERMO should be used and integrated into care processes. Beyond, it relies only on written text meaning that individuals with visual impairments or limited reading skills would be excluded from using this health intervention.

5 Characteristics of technology to achieve agency

The example provided descriptions of functionalities and technologies that are needed to support patient agency by health CAs. Table 1 maps the agency aspects from section 3 to the technologies required to achieve an impact and evaluation aspects from the health CA development and evaluation framework.

NLP and Natural Language Understanding (NLU) enables CAs to understand and interpret patient input accurately. Such understanding is needed to provide relevant and helpful responses when patients are using a health CA for accessing health information (C1). Additionally correct medical knowledge is required to let a CA provide health information. Eight aspects from the evaluation framework are related to these technological aspects that are relevant to ensure the quality of NLP and NLU including correctness of the provided information. Accessibility and usability of a CA are also essential for improving access to information.

Based on user preferences or user characteristics a CA can tailor advice and information to individual patient needs, preferences, and health histories. Presuming personalization or tailoring techniques are integrated in a CA (C2), CAs can empower patients to make informed decisions.

Health CAs can collect information from the user directly or from integrated sensors and monitoring technology (C3). In this way, the health status can be monitored and shown to the patient together with feedback by the CA. An active reporting of CA-requested health data into the chat (e.g. nutrition information) engages the patient and helps reflecting behavior. Additionally, feedback or reminders given by the CA integrate a patient into the care process. To benefit from this, user engagement is required, an aspect that is already in the evaluation framework.

Sentiment or emotions analysis technologies as well as NLP and NLU technologies are required for enabling a health CA to provide emotional support (C4). The framework includes three aspects necessary to realize high-level emotional support, namely understanding, empathy and linguistic accuracy. Similar to a patient-doctor relationship, also the patient-to-CA relationship should be characterized by trust. Good understanding of the patient's input by the CA is essential to create a trustful relationship. Additionally, ensuring the confidentiality and security of patient data is essential for building trust and encouraging honest and open communication, reflected by the aspect security in the framework.

An intuitive and easy-to-use interface is crucial for ensuring that patients of all ages, health literacy levels, reading skills and tech-savviness levels can interact effectively with the CA. Providing support in multiple languages as well multiple data entry and output options (e.g. voice recognition and speech-to-text) can enhance accessibility and comprehension for a diverse patient population (C5). We have two aspects in the evaluation framework addressing these factors: accessibility and ease of use.

6 Measuring Patient Agency

In the previous section, we identified aspects from the technological perspective that are prerequisites for achieving an impact on patient agency resulting from the usage of a health CA. However, we can recognize that this technological perspective is missing the human factors' perspective of patient agency. The human factors' perspective rather involves measuring how the interaction with a health CA impacts on a patient's ability to make informed decisions, to manage their health, and to actively participate in their care. To consider this facet also as part of the health CA evaluation and development framework (Denecke, 2023), we suggest to add an additional dimension, called "Human factors Perspective" and collected categories and metrics that can be used to measure impact of health CA usage on patient agency. They are summarized in the following linking them to the 5 characteristics of agency introduced in section 3 and shown in Table 2.

Improved access to health information and health literacy (C1) as well as tailored advice (C2) and patient engagement (C3) impact on health literacy, decision making confidence and self-management capabilities. Accordingly, we identified metrics that allow measuring these aspects: The Decision Self-Efficacy Scale measures the self-confidence or belief in one's ability to make decisions, including participation in shared decision making (O'Connor, 2002). The Health Literacy Questionnaire (HLQ) (Sørensen et al., 2013) assesses a patient's ability to understand health information and make informed decisions. The PAM-13 (Hibbard et al., 2005) measures self-reported knowledge, skill, and confidence for self-management of one's health or chronic condition.

Emotional support and trust (C4) could be considered as patient satisfaction with the treatment (Friedel et al., 2023). Patient-reported outcome measures (PROM) and patient-reported experience measures (PREM) are standard tools for measuring patients' perspectives on the care they receive, the treatment process, and related issues. PROM typically focuses on specific treatment outcomes through questionnaires, such as those assessing health-related quality of life. In contrast, PREM gather insights into patients' experiences of healthcare services and provides direct feedback to healthcare providers. This feedback is used to improve the system and promote integrative care.

Reducing healthcare barriers, i.e. the access to healthcare services is difficult to measure. It could be indirectly measured as health-related quality of life, e.g by SF-36 Hays et al. (1993) or EQ-5D (https://euroqol.org/) assuming that health-related quality of life increases when healthcare services can be accessed. SF-36 or EQ-5D can indirectly reflect patient agency by assessing how health status affects the patient's day-to-day life and perceived control over their health. EQ-5D is a well-known and widely used health status instrument (Devlin and Brooks, 2017). SF-36 (Ware et al., 1996) is a 36-item patient-reported survey of the health status.

7 Discussion

In this paper, we identified possible impacts of CAs in healthcare on patients' agency. They include improved access to health information, tailored advice, improved engagement, delivering emotional support and trust as well as reducing healthcare barriers (RQ1). We aggregated several technological aspects that are prerequisite for achieving these impacts on patient agency. They comprise NLP and NLU, sentiment and emotion analysis techniques integrated in health CAs, access to knowledge sources, personalization techniques, and monitoring technology (RQ2). To evaluate the impact

Table 1: Technology required to achieve an impact on the patient agency as well as relevant technical aspects from the health CA evaluation and development framework (Denecke, 2023)

Agency aspect	**Required technology**	**Aspects from the framework (Denecke, 2023)**
C1	Access to knowledge sources and integrated knowledge, understanding user needs, natural language processing (NLP) and natural language understanding (NLU) technologies	Accessibility, ease of use, content accuracy, linguistic accuracy, understanding, comprehensibility, flexibility, classifier performance
C2	Understanding user input, information on user characteristics and user preferences, personalization techniques	Context awareness, appropriateness of responses, understanding, security
C3	Monitoring technology, sensors, collecting user data, feedback mechanisms / reminders, interpretation of data	Engagement
C4	Sentiment or emotions analysis technologies, NLP and NLU technologies	Understanding, empathy, linguistic accuracy, security
C5	Easy-to-use interface, multilinguality, multiple data entry and output options	Accessibility, ease of use

Table 2: Human factors perspective together with evaluation aspects and metrics to be added to the CA evaluation and development framework (Denecke, 2023) to consider patient agency

Category	**Possible metrics**
Impact on self-management capabilities	Health Literacy Questionnaire (HLQ) (Sørensen et al., 2013), PAM-13 (Hibbard et al., 2005), Decision Self Efficacy Scale
Impact on patient satisfaction with treatment	PROM, PREM
Impact on access to healthcare services	Indirectly measured through health-related quality of life, e.g by SF-36 Hays et al. (1993) or EQ-5D (https://euroqol.org/

of CAs on patient agency, it should be assessed on the one hand whether the required technologies are available and of good quality, which could be realized by considering evaluation aspects of the health CA evaluation framework (RQ3) (Denecke, 2023).

On the other hand, for evaluating the impact of a health CA on the patient agency (RQ3), we identified examples of metrics that could be used to measure the impact of health CA usage on patient agency. For the single aspects such as quality of life or health literacy there exist multiple assessment tools. We only presented some examples of metrics that might be useful. More research is needed on testing whether these metrics and scales are useful to assess the impact of health CA interaction on the agency of a patient.

Our work has been optimistic in the sense that we believe in a positive impact of the use of health CAs on patient agency. However, there could be negative impacts if CAs hinder patient agency. Some examples are described in the following: If a CA's NLP capabilities are limited, it may struggle to understand and respond accurately to complex health queries, reducing its effectiveness and patient trust. Generic, one-size-fits-all responses may be less helpful and fail to address individual patient concerns, undermining patient agency. In previous studies it was found that users often do not know what to ask or write when addressing a health CA (Denecke et al., 2020a) which can be a significant barrier, especially for older or less tech-savvy persons. Providing outdated or inaccurate health information can lead to misinformed decisions, negatively impacting patient health and trust. If a CA cannot access or use existing patient health records, its advice may be less relevant or accurate. Concerns about data security and privacy can deter patients from sharing sensitive information, limiting the effectiveness of the CA. A lack of multilingual support can exclude non-native speakers or those with limited knowledge of the CA's operating language. CAs that fail to recognize or respond appropriately to health emergencies can pose significant risks to patient safety (Denecke et al., 2019).

Furthermore, patients may become overly reliant on CAs for health information and decision-making, leading to reduced engagement in their own health management and critical thinking about their health choices. If a CA provides information that is too complex, inaccurate, or not context-specific, patients might misinterpret it. This misunderstanding could lead to poor health decisions. Over-dependence on CAs might lead to reduced interaction with healthcare professionals, which can be detrimental. Human elements like empathy, experience-based intuition, and detailed understanding of a patient's history are critical for effective healthcare. If the algorithms driving the CA are biased, the information and recommendations provided could be skewed, leading to unequal and potentially harmful guidance for certain patient groups. Technical issues like errors in understanding language, limited response capabilities, or system downtime can lead to frustration and reduced patient confidence in managing their health. CAs providing too much information, or information that is not prioritized based on the patient's immediate needs, can overwhelm patients, making it challenging for them to make informed decisions.

In addition, research on health CA has shown that their design, including complexity of responses and persona, significantly influences their effectiveness in providing health information (Biro et al., 2023). However, concerns about accuracy, cybersecurity, and the inability of AI-led services to empathize may compromise patient engagement with CA (Nadarzynski et al., 2019). These examples show that there is a huge need to systematically assess impact of health CAs on patient agency. Our research therefore contributes a first step towards ensuring that health CA have a positive impact on patient agency. Clearly , it is based on experiences and needs validation and extension in future.

8 Conclusions

In this paper, we assessed how health CA can impact on patient agency. By focusing exclusively on patients' agency - rather than that of healthcare professionals - this paper contributes to the growing discourse on patient-centered technology in healthcare, and offers insights and recommendations for the future development and implementation of CA. We conclude that, provided the appropriate technology is chosen, health CAs can have an impact on patient agency, but careful design is needed to achieve such impact and to ensure a positive impact on agency. Typically, studies of health CAs examine their effectiveness in relation to a health outcome or usability. Research is needed to understand which technologies have which effects on agency. Studies measuring the impact on patient agency are still lacking and has to be done in future.

References

Serena Barello, Guendalina Graffigna, Elena Vegni, et al. 2012. Patient engagement as an emerging challenge for healthcare services: mapping the literature. *Nursing research and practice*, 2012.

Mary Bates. 2019. Health care chatbots are here to help. *IEEE pulse*, 10(3):12–14.

Joshua Biro, Courtney Linder, David Neyens, et al. 2023. The effects of a health care chatbot's complexity and persona on user trust, perceived usability, and effectiveness: mixed methods study. *JMIR Human Factors*, 10(1):e41017.

Amanda Bok, Declan Noone, and Naja Skouw-Rasmussen. 2022. Patient agency: key questions and challenges–a report from the 1st workshop of the ehc think tank workstream on patient agency. *The Journal of Haemophilia Practice*, 9(1):27–35.

Kerstin Denecke. 2023. Framework for guiding the development of high-quality conversational agents in healthcare. In *Healthcare*, volume 11, page 1061. MDPI.

Kerstin Denecke, Richard May, and Yihan Deng. 2019. Towards emotion-sensitive conversational user interfaces in healthcare applications. *Studies in Health Technology and Informatics*, 264:1164–1168.

Kerstin Denecke, Richard May, Annkathrin Pöpel, and Sandra Lutz Hochreutener. 2020a. Can a chatbot increase the motivation to provide personal health information? *Studies in health technology and informatics*, 273:85–90.

Kerstin Denecke, Sayan Vaaheesan, and Aaganya Arulnathan. 2020b. A mental health chatbot for regulating emotions (sermo) – concept and usability test. *Transactions on Emerging Topics in Computing*, 9(3):1170–1182.

Nancy J Devlin and Richard Brooks. 2017. Eq-5d and the euroqol group: past, present and future. *Applied health economics and health policy*, 15:127–137.

Anna Lena Friedel, Sonja Siegel, Cedric Fabian Kirstein, Monja Gerigk, Ulrike Bingel, Anke Diehl, Oliver Steidle, Steffen Haupeltshofer, Bernhard Andermahr, Witold Chmielewski, et al. 2023. Measuring patient experience and patient satisfaction—how are we doing it and why does it matter? a comparison of european and us american approaches. In *Healthcare*, volume 11, page 797. MDPI.

Floriana Gashi, Selina F Regli, Richard May, Philipp Tschopp, and Kerstin Denecke. 2021. Developing intelligent interviewers to collect the medical history: Lessons learned and guidelines. In *dHealth*, pages 18–25. IOS Press.

Ron D Hays, Cathy Donald Sherbourne, and Rebecca M Mazel. 1993. The rand 36-item health survey 1.0. *Health economics*, 2(3):217–227.

Judith H Hibbard, Eldon R Mahoney, Jean Stockard, and Martin Tusler. 2005. Development and testing of a short form of the patient activation measure. *Health services research*, 40(6p1):1918–1930.

Judy Hunter, Margaret Franken, and Deborah Balmer. 2015. Constructions of patient agency in healthcare settings: textual and patient perspectives. *Discourse, Context & Media*, 7:37–44.

Amanda L Joseph, Andre W Kushniruk, and Elizabeth M Borycki. 2020. Patient journey mapping: current practices, challenges and future opportunities in healthcare. *Knowledge management & e-learning*, 12(4):387.

Ahmet B Kocaballi, Shlomo Berkovsky, Juan C Quiroz, Liliana Laranjo, Huong L Tong, Dana Rezazadegan, Agustina Briatore, and Enrico Coiera. 2019. The personalization of conversational agents in health care: systematic review. *Journal of Medical Internet Research*, 21(11):e15360.

Dillys Larbi, Kerstin Denecke, and Elia Gabarron. 2022. Usability testing of a social media chatbot for increasing physical activity behavior. *Journal of Personalized Medicine*, 12(5):828.

Richard May and Kerstin Denecke. 2020. Extending patient education with claire: An interactive virtual reality and voice user interface application. In *EC-TEL*, pages 482–486.

Jingbo Meng and Yue Dai. 2021. Emotional support from ai chatbots: Should a supportive partner self-disclose or not? *Journal of Computer-Mediated Communication*, 26(4):207–222.

Tom Nadarzynski, Oliver Miles, Aimee Cowie, and Damien Ridge. 2019. Acceptability of artificial intelligence (ai)-led chatbot services in healthcare: A mixed-methods study. *Digital Health*, 5:2055207619871808.

Tom Nadarzynski, Vannesa Puentes, Izabela Pawlak, Tania Mendes, Ian Montgomery, Jake Bayley, Damien Ridge, and Christy Newman. 2021. Barriers and facilitators to engagement with artificial intelligence (ai)-based chatbots for sexual and reproductive health advice: a qualitative analysis. *Sexual health*, 18(5):385–393.

Annette M O'Connor. 2002. Decision self-efficacy scale. *APA PsycTests*.

Dan O'Hair, Melinda M Villagran, Elaine Wittenberg, Kenneth Brown, Monica Ferguson, Harry T Hall, and Timothy Doty. 2003. Cancer survivorship and agency model: implications for patient choice, decision making, and influence. *Health Communication*, 15(2):193–202.

Kristine Sørensen, Stephan Van den Broucke, Jürgen M Pelikan, James Fullam, Gerardine Doyle, Zofia Slonska, Barbara Kondilis, Vivian Stoffels, Richard H Osborne, and Helmut Brand. 2013. Measuring health literacy in populations: illuminating the design and development process of the european health literacy survey questionnaire (hls-eu-q). *BMC public health*, 13:1–10.

Richard L Street Jr, Gregory Makoul, Neeraj K Arora, and Ronald M Epstein. 2009. How does communication heal? pathways linking clinician–patient communication to health outcomes. *Patient education and counseling*, 74(3):295–301.

Mauro Tschanz, Tim L Dorner, Jürgen Holm, and Kerstin Denecke. 2018. Using emma to manage medication. *Computer*, 51(8):18–25.

John E Ware, KK Snow, M Kosinski, and B Gandek. 1996. The sf-36 health survey. *Manual and interpretation guide*, 2.

Why academia should cut back on general enthusiasm about CAs

Alessia Giulimondi
Utrecht University
a.giulimondi@students.uu.nl

Abstract

This position paper will analyze LLMs, the core technology of CAs, from a socio-technical and linguistic perspective in order to argue for a limitation of its use in academia, which should be reflected in a more cautious adoption of CAs in private spaces.

The article describes how machine learning technologies like LLMs are inserted into a more general process of platformization, negatively affecting autonomy of research. Moreover, fine-tuning practices, as means to polish language models are questioned, explaining how these foster a deterministic approach to language.

A leading role of universities in this general gain of awareness is strongly advocated, as institutions that support transparent and open science, in order to foster and protect democratic values in our societies.

1 Introduction

Ever since the deployment to the general public of Chat-GPT, the public debate has promptly polarized around an excessive enthusiasm or an equally disproportioned alarm toward systems like Conversational Agents (hereafter CAs), that employ a technology supported either partially or entirely by machine learning algorithms. Recognizing a frequent failure in identifying the strong continuity these technologies manifest with their predecessors, this position paper will try to connect to each other the very diversified criticalities of the deployment of these technologies to identify the risks they pose for individual and institutional autonomy.

This position paper will focus on a specific class of deep learning architectures, Large Language Models (LLM), since they represent the core technology that constitutes Conversational Agents (CAs). This paper will advocate that specifically academia, given its (in principle) neutral position in society, in between and above interests of the market and the necessities of the state and its government, should take a clear stand for the limitation of LLMs, as industry-driven technologies, in its domain of competence (i.e. universities, research institutes). By doing so, academia may be able to influence society regarding its judgement and attituted toward devices such as CA that in most cases rely on LLMs.

Relying on LLMs, CA belong to those technologies developed and deployed by American high-tech private companies and growing literature (Van Dijck et al., 2023; Van Dijck, 2021; Benn and Lazar, 2022; Tafani, 2022; Hovy and Spruit, 2016) is showing the serious ethical and socio-technical problematics of a technological development that increasingly witnesses a concentration of power in a few private enterprises. Moreover, various comprehensive analyses have highlighted the negative effects of LLMs and data collection and profiling practices more in general (Couldry and Mejias, 2019; Weidinger et al., 2022; Matz et al., 2023; Andrić and Kasirzadeh, 2023). However, the alarming implications of these studies for individual and institutional autonomy, despite authors do not abstain to account for them, are too often underestimated.

It is sensible to argue that this general attitude to consider of secondary importance the warnings of scholars, technicians and activists (Chomsky, 2023; Harari, 2018) about the dangers of a techno-economic monopoly and user profiling undermines the soundness of technological development itself, as well as the integrity and autonomy of public research institutions (Kersessens and van Dijck, 2022). Indeed, autonomy of universities is crucial to ensure that democratic values are preserved in a society. Nevertheless, critiques to the current modalities of technological development are often casted aside, mostly perceived as a major impediment to the progress of society (Tafani, 2022) – arguably implying an understanding of progress only driven and substantiated by technical advance-

Proceedings of the 1st Worskhop on Towards Ethical and Inclusive Conversational AI: Language Attitudes, Linguistic Diversity, and Language Rights (TEICAI 2024), pages 9–15
March 22, 2024

ment.

Universities should foster and protect free, autonomous and creative research as a foundational value of its existence, resulting in a natural opposition to any policy, favored by the implementation of specific designs of a technology, that hinders in any way the free practice of autonomous scientific inquiry. Indeed, it is important to recognize how philosophical reflections, promoted by autonomous academic research, must sustain technological development, by ensuring a solid base for ethical decisions that (should) have the ultimate say in the deployment to the society at large of technically complex tools intended to serve and support (when not replace) very diverse human activities.

This article will describe the dependency of LLMs from a platform society (2.1) to argue for a lack of autonomy of research in the presence of a techno-economic monopoly. Section 2.2 will describe how this results in a structural dependency of academia from big tech companies and section 2.3 will argue for the inappropriateness of the use of opaque technologies in academic research. In section 3 the processes involved in fine-tuning will be outlined to question the validity of models that propose a deterministic and one-sided view of language. Thus, a critical analysis of the implications of leaving to private companies the modeling of language and the use of these models to generate language in robots or devices (e.g. CAs) is proposed. By evaluating the critical characteristics of CAs through the examination of the problematics of LLMs, this paper will advocate for the necessity of academia to assume a leading role in the identification of the dangers of the dominating trends of technological development, to favor a shift toward more democratic ones.

2 LLM and CAs as an opaque product of a platform society

2.1 Platformization

Research conducted by José van Dijck in the last decade is of fundamental importance to gain a complete picture of the socio-technical context in which LLMs and CAs are developed.

What van Dijck proposes is an analysis of the recent socio-political and socio-economic changes within the frame of a platformization process, a process that is transforming our societies as industrialization did in the past. Platformization is described as a dynamic that happens within a platform ecosystem, understood as "a corporate space" (Van Dijck et al., 2023, p .3441) that is commonly known to be controlled by five American private companies (Google, Apple, Facebook, Amazon, Microsoft, GAFAM). This ecosystem is a socio-technical infrastructure that is able to penetrate the public and private spheres, increasing the dependence of the latter on their services. Van Dijck described the complex dynamics that govern this platform ecosystem, "hierarchical and proprietary in nature" (Van Dijck et al., 2023, p .3441) as a data-driven system which survives nourished by a continuous collection of data. This ecosystem presents a layered structure of three levels where the Big Five have been increasing their presence and control. The deeper level of the infrastructure is constituted by underwater cables and data centers that ensure the collection and distribution of data, while the intermediate level includes the cloud services necessary to process the data. The sectoral applications (e.g. mobility or educational apps) depend on these "lower" infrastructures and the vertical integration across the three levels of infrastructures. Increasing the dominance of private corporations in the deeper level and the intermediate level is resulting in an overall privatization of the Internet space which was initially intended to overcome the geopolitical barriers and interests to serve as a "utility, independently organized and managed" (Van Dijck et al., 2023, p.2805).

Therefore, proposing an analysis that considers the advent of Artificial Intelligence in strict continuity with this progressive and accelerated penetration of private infrastructures into spheres that traditionally belong to the public domain is perhaps not ventured. Indeed, van Dijck points out how a specific feature of this ecosystem is its capability of posing itself outside of the traditional limits of the public and private spheres. In other words, this companies built a system which survives on the exceptionality of their position within the civil society, making laws and regulations hard to be applied. "Tech companies deliberately push their platforms to vacillate between sectors and infrastructures, between markets and nonmarkets, between private and public interests, between a marketplace for goods and services and a marketplace of ideas, while adopting features of both." (Van Dijck, 2021, p. 2810)

2.2 A structural dependency

The deployment to the public of Chat-GPT falls under this well-established process of releasing technologies that are nurtured in their roots by the monopolizing nature of the system that created them (Van Dijck, 2021). This ecosystem sustains itself by datafication, strictly connected and dependent on the platformization described in 2.1. Datafication is the process of transforming activities performed online into data-points exploitable by private and/or public companies and institutions, and it is the result of the seamless flow of data across the three layers of the system, which ensures a solid control of the entire infrastructure that supports data collection and distribution (Couldry and Mejias, 2019). Eventually, this made possible for tech companies to gather data deep enough to train a model that has enough parameters (or weights) to perform surprisingly well in NLP and language generation, paving the way for more human-like CAs (Couldry and Mejias, 2019). However, it is important to mention studies that have recently shown how it is possible to have seemingly performant language models that rely on smaller datasets (van Dijk et al., 2023). Thus, it is perhaps possible to imagine artificial neural networks that do not necessarily rely on immense quantity of human data. Nevertheless, it is generally acknowledged the monopoly of the Big Five in the development and deployment of LLMs, which naturally draws the attention of researchers concerned about the ethical implications of these models to the ones that are most commonly used in both private and public contexts. The benignity of some language models trained independently, on non-opaque datasets with transparent methodologies in the pre-training and fine-tuning phases do not fall in the scope of this paper. It is the monopoly of tech-companies over LLMs and the consequent imposition of their theoretical assumptions and designs what poses serious concerns for the autonomy of research, since in the majority of cases universities have to rely at least on the pre-training phases provided by private tech companies (Kersessens and van Dijck, 2022). The power gained in the last decades by GAFAM across the layers of the digital infrastructure makes the creation of an independent system extremely costly (Karpathy, 2023) and ostensibly less efficient for any small tech enterprise whether private or funded by the university or the government.

This is a first direct influence of private corporations over public educational institutions, such as the university. Through the appropriation of expertise and infrastructures, they offer researchers (as well as private users) the only choice of selecting one of the few companies that are able to provide highly performing digital services (from software and cloud services to language models like Chat-GPT), inevitably "imposing their architecture choice design upon users" (Van Dijck, 2021, p. 2810). This architecture choice becomes an imposition in absence of a fair market in which a truly diversified range of possibilities is offered to users and institutions. Moreover, it becomes an even more unsettling scenario when the freedom itself for institutions to build their own platforms, that abide to the rules decided within that institution, is heavily limited by the privatization of the infrastructures of the Internet. Therefore, a first direct impact on autonomy of research is arguably observable when a specific architecture for LLMs is deployed and researchers are urged to adopt them, often mostly on the basis of their performativity. It is possible to counterargument that it is in the very nature of research employing the best tools available on the market for ends that might be beneficial for research itself and for society at large. However, this view heavily undermines the freedom of scientific inquiry that, in principle, should not become entirely dependent on companies primarily driven by interest of profit, in order not to erode the fundamental difference between academic research and industrial research (Kersessens and van Dijck, 2022).

2.3 LLMs: an opaque technology

A second aspect that should be taken into consideration when talking about CAs and their use in both private and public spheres is that LLMs, their core technologies, rely on data collection and processing that are notably opaque in their nature (Vetrò et al., 2019; Couldry and Mejias, 2019; Tafani, 2022; Andrić and Kasirzadeh, 2023). The creation of parameters (or weights) during the training stage of these larger models (e.g. Chat- GPT, Llama, Gemini) is arguably one of the most controversial part, as this is the stage where researchers admit the lowest level of control over the process. Andrej Karphaty, in one of his lectures, explains clearly how artificial neural networks are treated by computer scientists involved in their development as "mostly inscrutable, empirical artifacts" (Karpathy, 2023). Therefore, a structural opaqueness lies at the core of larger LLMs and this already poses some concerns about the appropriateness of employing such artifacts as tools intended to support academic research, while valuing transparency as a fundamental principle for a more open science. A straightforward example of the negative repercussions of this opacity (together with a frequency-driven nature of the model) is that "LMs are trained to predict the *likelihood* of utterances", which does not predict its correctness and "this may present a theoretical limit on LM capabilities to detect misinformation" (Weidinger et al., 2022, p. 218). Furthermore, it was shown how this opaqueness does not conform to privacy regulations and democratic principles that constitute the foundations of substantial freedom in democratic societies (Weidinger et al., 2022; Andrić and Kasirzadeh, 2023; Couldry and Mejias, 2019). Thus, universities and research institutes that support democratic values within a society have the social responsibility to limit, at least within its direct domain of actions, the indiscriminate adoption of highly controversial technologies on the socio-technical and socio-economic level.

It is also true, however, how a first, crucial, step toward this desirable academic policy is to recognize the controversial status of these technologies. Nevertheless, due to the blurred distinction between public and private sectors created within this platform ecosystem (see 2.1), it is often not easy also for researchers to spot the ambiguities and criticalities of these processes, as university and research more in general are themselves part of this process of platformization (Kersessens and van Dijck, 2022). Indeed, the lack of awareness of university's overreliance on Big Tech companies' infrastructures and services appears to be a rather established phenomenon, as it is demonstrated by the regular practice to use Google Scholar as a starting point of any literature search, which lies at the foundations of any scientific investigation. The implications for diversity of the literature and the consequent autonomy of scientific studies are rarely sounded out.

Thus, to conclude this first section, it is reasonable to view LLMs and CAs as a general phenomenon of strengthening the dominance of big tech companies in both public and private sectors (including academia) and a natural continuation of the development of technologies that mostly follow the logics of the market. In the following section, we will analyze how the socio-political problematics highlighted in this first part of the article cannot be completely separated from the more technical concerns that can be raised regarding the development of language models, that follow the structures and logics of a commercial company.

3 Modeling language for machine learning: is it really appropriate?

In linguistic research, the practice of creating language models is uncontroversial and largely employed to propose and explain theories of language. Models enable us to visualize and better understand the mechanisms of phenomena like language that are not directly accessible via simple observations and descriptions. We need theories and hypotheses to model language and we need models to argue for those same theories and hypotheses. A good definition of a scientific model is the one that defines it as a "visualization of entities non representable in other ways, in their reduction to an empirical description, in the simulation of the logico-structural characteristics of a research object, via the creation of isomorphisms and analogies." ('modello', 2023). van Dijk et al.'s (2023), explains the large potential these language models have for research in language acquisition, as they represent a statistical model that informs us of the possibilities of statistical learning likely at play in language acquisition. Set aside the ethical controversies connected to the use of opaque systems, this can be an overall correct use of a language model. Indeed, in this type of research scenario, the language model would serve the role of a model that supports the scientific understanding of reality (language acquisition, in this case). On the other hand, when (large) Language Models are fed into a system created specifically to interact with humans, like in the case of CAs, the situation substantially changes. Firstly, the model, initially intended as a hypothetical approximation of how language works, becomes a generative system that is meant to imitate a natural, human phenomenon like speaking. More concretely, CAs are intended to use a language that meets syntactic, pragmatic and discourse standards that are inevitably decided by their developers (Karpathy, 2023; Kasirzadeh and Gabriel, 2023). These standards are manually inserted during the fine-tuning process, which needs human intervention to categorize responses that are considered appropriate or correct. The problem of this common practice, known as Reinforcement Learning from Human Feedback (RLHF), is the aprioristic choice that lies beneath any categorization of this kind. Indeed, LLMs undergo two phases of their training: the first one (pre-training) where parameters are created and fed into the neural network and the second phase, which prepares the model to be able to answer questions. This second phase consists of a process called fine-tuning. Fine-tuning makes use of labels that have to be assigned to different types of potential responses a CA can give to the user. This is meant to make a first alignment to human conversational conventions, by teaching the algorithm which responses are more desirable or more correct. Fine-tuning is commonly the phase where researchers try to operate most interventions (Kasirzadeh and Gabriel, 2023) to reduce toxicity, inappropriateness and biases of the model often shown to be a major issue for social discrimination and perpetuation of stereotypes (Weidinger et al., 2022; Andrić and Kasirzadeh, 2023). However, the question of whether it is really possible to clean these models from biases and what this really entails is often avoided. In a recent talk held at the Symposium of philosophy of science, AI and machine learning, Tom Sterkenburg described how biases are rather natural outcomes of LLMs because of the naturally biased nature of human data on which they are trained (Sterkenburg, 2023). Moreover, he also explained how this biases are also model-dependent. Thus, it is perhaps a "false problem" to talk about biases in LLMs, and focusing the large part of AI ethic research on the removal of biases that cannot ultimately be removed risks to be counterproductive. Nevertheless, what it seems even more crucial in order to understand the need for a change in perspective is to further analyze the implications of this "fight" against biases of the algorithms. Kasirzadeh and Gabriel's (2023) proposed an application of the knowledge of pragmatics to CAs, employing Gricean maxims and Speech Act theory to elaborate a set of rules that an ideal CA should follow in order to be a desirable conversational partner. The elaboration of these rules are intended to propose a pragmatic approach for the long-standing problem of what can be considered a human value general enough to be universally extended. However, the proposal only succeeds in demonstrating the methodological inadequacy of applying linguistic theory to commercial products meant to be used by a wide variety of people in a large set of diversified contexts. Linguistic theories, such as Speech Act theory and Grice maxims (Huang, 2016; Mabaquiao, 2018) do not have to be understood as rules humans have to follow to have a successful conversation. Rather, they were proposed to describe conventions and general patterns that are hypothesized to be at play in human linguistic interactions. Thus, they should not be understood as directly applicable to automated processes. Indeed, the essential problematic of CAs is the automation that lies at the core of its functioning. Automating a process such as language, which linguists still struggle to understand as a phenomenon and which manifests itself as a creative, continuously changing and evolving process is intrinsically problematic. Automating it on the base of a model mostly grounded on statistical probabilities and a subsequent labeling process may easily lead to a deterministic view of language, with non-negligible consequences for autonomy of the user repeatedly exposed to a pre-determined language. This approach is in line with a more general approach, often referred to as a "new behaviorism" (Tafani, 2022). In this regard, we signal the thorough analysis conducted by Benn and Lazar's (2022) about Automated Influence.

Therefore, the problem does not resolve itself on the decision of which type of labels is best to assign, but the concerns lay on the very nature of the labeling process necessary for fine-tuning. Indeed, labeling excerpts of texts can endanger freedom of thought and expression, as it implicitly conveys what is allowed and what is better avoid saying. This can be argued from evidence we have from speech alignment (Pickering and Garrod, 2004) that showed how interlocutors tend to align to the language of their addressee on various linguistic levels (syntactic, lexical, phonological, pragmatic). Thus, it is reasonable to hypothesize that a similar pattern of alignment can occur also when the interlocutor is not human, but it successfully imitates human language. The intention here is not to argue for a direct impact of CAs on users, as in an online alignment to the CA which eventually results in a permanent alteration of language use of the individual user. There is no scientific basis to hypothesize such an outcome. The purpose of this last consideration is rather highlighting how speech alignment studies can inform us about the capacity language has to shape and modify itself and its environment according to necessities and contexts, and how this is directly linked to how humans adapt and adjust depending on the situations and interlocutors. Thus, it is important to critically understand what it means to engage in various conversations with devices that successfully resemble human language, while this resemblance is a product of very different mechanisms from the ones that operate in the human brain (van Dijk et al., 2023). Indeed, one of the inherent characteristics of human language is precisely the capacity of creating an infinite set of possible outputs given a finite set of items (Hauser et al., 2002). Setting aside the fact that the state of LLMs seems to resemble quite the opposite situation, the free creation of linguistic material, highly interrelated with thought generation and its free expression, can be seriously challenged by a view that considers language a large set of items that can be labeled according to pragmatic conventions, wrongly interpreted as rules to follow, and policies that set standards for what it can be considered civil to say. Thus, more research is needed that addresses this issue, *before* deploying to the public technologies of which the long-terms effects are mostly unknown.

It is now, perhaps, easier to understand why the problems with language modeling are also deeply interrelated with the fact that LLMs that are more commonly used are mostly developed by private corporations that are inevitably imposing a unilateral, English-centered and Western-centered model of language – for obvious reasons connected to the centralization of tech-power in American companies described above. Therefore, it is not easy to disentangle the problems inherent to language models and problems related to the monopoly over these by GAFAM. In other words, it is difficult to research LLMs and their design with sufficient objectivity, if what is currently mostly available on the market is only one way of doing things (with few variations).

Freeing machine learning technologies from a monopoly that interests a large portion of the globe is crucial to ensure enough diversity in technological research and development, which is at the foundation of effective and meaningful research intended to benefit society as a whole. Researchers in the field of linguistics, data and computer science, electronic engineering, philosophers, psychologists and sociologists should be able to conduct their individual and collaborative work independently, both from a socio-psychological perspective and technical perspective. Indeed, they should not be dependent on private companies for the delivery of tools and expertise, nor they should suffer from an imposition of a specific design of language and interaction, mostly designed to induce the user to stay hooked to the device (Matz et al., 2023; Hovy and Spruit, 2016; Couldry and Mejias, 2019).

In order for societies and governments to envision these problematics and promote practices and regulations that support an open and democratic technological advancement, it is essential that the university, as a social party that historically fosters diversity of thought and free creation and circulation of knowledge, takes a clear stand in the limitation of the expansion of highly controversial technologies in research and society.

4 Limitations and conclusions

As it was already pointed out by van Dijk et al.'s (2023), deep learning technologies are a "moving target" considering the fast pace at which their training and deployment is moving. For this reason, it is not possible to discuss the abilities LLMs will have in some months. However, this state of the art should prompt academia to reflect once again on the appropriateness and overall safety of this general acceleration, driven by unconstrained release of technologies by private companies that puts researchers in serious difficulties when attempting to investigate with lucidity and transparency these tools.

Moreover, it is not among the intentions of this article to deny the numerous benefits LLMs may have for research. Indeed, the implicit proposal of this dissertation is the distinction between LLMs used for research purposes – once ensured autonomy, fairness and transparency – and LLMs implemented in CAs, meant to be used by private users for different goals. Within this distinction, benefits for research are positively reviewed, while benefits for the private user are questioned. Furthermore, the fine-tuning practices largely employed with an intention to improve the model and polish it from biases and toxicity are critically reviewed. It is, indeed, proposed a view that questions the validity of automation of language from a methodological perspective, arguing that it supports a deterministic approach to linguistic data and human behavior more in general.

Finally, we limit our critique to LLMs that employ parameters and architectures financed, developed and/or supported by private corporations that hold a great asymmetric power with public institutions and governments across the globe. Whether this interests the vast majority of LLMs currently used, it is left to the judgement of the reader.

References

Katja Andrić and Atoosa Kasirzadeh. 2023. Reconciling Governmental Use of Online Targeting With Democracy. In *Proceedings of the 2023 ACM Conference on Fairness, Accountability, and Transparency*, FAccT '23, pages 1871–1881, New York, NY, USA. Association for Computing Machinery.

Claire Benn and Seth Lazar. 2022. What's Wrong with Automated Influence. *Canadian Journal of Philosophy*, 52(1):125–148. Publisher: Cambridge University Press.

Noam Chomsky. 2023. Opinion | Noam Chomsky: The False Promise of ChatGPT.

Nick Couldry and Ulises A. Mejias. 2019. Data Colonialism: Rethinking Big Data's Relation to the Contemporary Subject. *Television & New Media*, 20(4):336–349. Publisher: SAGE Publications.

Yuval Noah Harari. 2018. Why Technology Favors Tyranny. *The Atlantic*. Section: Technology.

Marc D. Hauser, Noam Chomsky, and W. Tecumseh Fitch. 2002. The faculty of language: what is it, who has it, and how did it evolve? In Hiroko Yamakido, Richard K. Larson, and Viviane Déprez, editors, *The Evolution of Human Language: Biolinguistic Perspectives*, Approaches to the Evolution of Language, pages 14–42. Cambridge University Press, Cambridge.

Dirk Hovy and Shannon L. Spruit. 2016. The Social Impact of Natural Language Processing. In *Proceedings of the 54th Annual Meeting of the Association for Computational Linguistics (Volume 2: Short Papers)*, pages 591–598, Berlin, Germany. Association for Computational Linguistics.

Yan Huang. 2016. Conversational Implicature.

Andrej Karpathy. 2023. [1hr Talk] Intro to Large Language Models [Video].

Atoosa Kasirzadeh and Iason Gabriel. 2023. In Conversation with Artificial Intelligence: Aligning language Models with Human Values. *Philosophy & Technology*, 36(2):27.

Neils Kersessens and José van Dijck. 2022. Governed by Edtech? Valuing Pedagogical Autonomy in a Platform Society. *Harvard Educational Review*, 92(2):284–303.

Napoleon Jr Mabaquiao. 2018. Speech act theory: From austin to searle. 19:35–45.

Sandra Matz, Jake Teeny, Sumer S. Vaid, Gabriella M. Harari, and Moran Cerf. 2023. The Potential of Generative AI for Personalized Persuasion at Scale. Publisher: OSF.

'modello'. 2023. Treccani.

Martin J. Pickering and Simon Garrod. 2004. The interactive-alignment model: Developments and refinements. *Behavioral and Brain Sciences*, 27(2):212–225. Publisher: Cambridge University Press.

Tom Sterkenburg. 2023. Epistemology and theory of machine learning.

Daniela Tafani. 2022. What's wrong with "AI ethics" narratives. Publisher: Zenodo Version Number: Published.

José Van Dijck. 2021. Seeing the forest for the trees: Visualizing platformization and its governance. *New Media & Society*, 23(9):2801–2819. Publisher: SAGE Publications.

José Van Dijck, Tim de Winkel, and Mirko Tobias Schäfer. 2023. Deplatformization and the governance of the platform ecosystem. *New Media & Society*, 25(12):3438–3454. Publisher: SAGE Publications.

Bram M. A. van Dijk, Tom Kouwenhoven, Marco R. Spruit, and Max J. van Duijn. 2023. Large Language Models: The Need for Nuance in Current Debates and a Pragmatic Perspective on Understanding. ArXiv:2310.19671 [cs].

Antonio Vetrò, Antonio Santangelo, Elena Beretta, and Juan Carlos De Martin. 2019. AI: from rational agents to socially responsible agents. *Digital Policy, Regulation and Governance*, 21(3):291–304. Publisher: Emerald Publishing Limited.

Laura Weidinger, Jonathan Uesato, Maribeth Rauh, Conor Griffin, Po-Sen Huang, John Mellor, Amelia Glaese, Myra Cheng, Borja Balle, Atoosa Kasirzadeh, Courtney Biles, Sasha Brown, Zac Kenton, Will Hawkins, Tom Stepleton, Abeba Birhane, Lisa Anne Hendricks, Laura Rimell, William Isaac, Julia Haas, Sean Legassick, Geoffrey Irving, and Iason Gabriel. 2022. Taxonomy of Risks posed by Language Models. In *2022 ACM Conference on Fairness, Accountability, and Transparency*, pages 214–229, Seoul Republic of Korea. ACM.

Bridging the Language Gap: Integrating Language Variations into Conversational AI Agents for Enhanced User Engagement

Marcellus Amadeus
Stanford University / São Paulo, Brazil
7marcellus@gmail.com

José Roberto Homeli da Silva
University of São Paulo / São Paulo, Brazil
jose.homeli.silva@alumni.usp.br

João Victor Pessoa Rocha
Federal University of Minas Gerais / Belo Horizonte, Brazil
joaovcpr@ufmg.br

Abstract

This paper presents the initial steps taken to integrate language variations into conversational AI agents to enhance user engagement. The study is built upon sociolinguistic and pragmatic traditions and involves the creation of an annotation taxonomy. The taxonomy includes eleven classes, ranging from concrete to abstract, and the covered aspects are the instance itself, time, sentiment, register, state, region, type, grammar, part of speech, meaning, and language. The paper discusses the challenges of incorporating vernacular language into AI agents, the procedures for data collection, and the taxonomy organization. It also outlines the next steps, including the database expansion and the computational implementation. The authors believe that integrating language variation into conversational AI will build near-real language inventories and boost user engagement. The paper concludes by discussing the limitations and the importance of building rapport with users through their own vernacular.

1 Introduction

Conversational agents have become more widespread among end users in recent years. Skjuve et al. (2022) explained that conversational agents are expected to have "intelligent" behavior and create relationships with users. Apple's Siri and Amazon's Alexa are great examples of how we interact with conversational AI.

To foster effective communication and rapport, speaking in a similar manner to AI users is imperative. Vernacular is the spoken language style through which people communicate when they are relaxed, and their level of monitoring is low (Wardhaugh, 2005). Thus, conversational AI professionals should strive to incorporate the target user's vernacular into their agent inventory. Our efforts go in the direction of how AI agents can respond in the target dialect. For instance, if a chatbot is set up to talk and write as a *Paulista*,[1] which lexical items and phrases would be relevant and representative of the *Paulista* dialect?

For that reason, this paper aims to outline the Language Variation Project at Alana AI (not operating anymore), which encompasses creating a database of expressions from Brazilian Portuguese (PT-BR) vernacular, especially those that vary according to the region and situation. As Labov informally stated, we understand variation as "different ways of saying the same thing" (Guy et al., 2007). Ultimately, it will be possible to use this database of expressions to build some sort of synonymy dictionary, enabling the AI agent to adapt its language according to the target end user's dialect. Further applicability of this labeled data involves using it as an instruction dataset that allows for fine-tuning a Large Language Model (LLM).

This study is organized as follows: in section 2 a brief discussion about language variation and AI is made; next, section 3 lists the procedures for data collection; in the section 4, we present the annotation taxonomy; and finally, we discuss expectations for the next steps of the project.

2 Related Work

Considered the father of modern Sociolinguistics, Labov asserted that, to understand language structure, linguists should study language variation in its social context (Agnihotri, 2013). Language variation is influenced by several elements, and one of

[1]Demonym to someone who was born in the state of São Paulo, Brazil.

Proceedings of the 1st Worskhop on Towards Ethical and Inclusive Conversational AI: Language Attitudes, Linguistic Diversity, and Language Rights (TEICAI 2024) , pages 16–20

them is social change. For instance, there are significant differences in speech between citizens from the state of Minas Gerais (Brazil) and those from the state of Santa Catarina (Brazil). This contrast happens due to the influence of cultural, geographical, and historical elements in their language.

Moreover, variation is a complex linguistic process. It can be multi-layered in the sense that it affects all language subsets: idiolects ("individual"), registers ("situational"), sociolects (group), dialects (region), and languages. Finegan and Biber (1994) went further and explained that the same patterns that motivate register variation also prompt sociolectal variation.

Therefore, our focus was on diatopic and diaphasic variation. Diatopic variation refers to the language variation related to geographical region differences, which is highly related to dialects; for example, the previously mentioned contrast between Minas Gerais and Santa Catarina. From another perspective, diaphasic variation[2] concerns the variation that is established depending on the communicative context (Raso and Mello, 2012); for instance, the distinction between formal and informal situations.

Implementing these processes into a conversational AI is highly challenging. Chaves et al. (2019) discussed a case study in which they implemented register analysis in order to help a chatbot understand how to speak to the user, and they concluded that the user reaction was better after the implementation. On the other hand, LLMs can fail with low frequency or new regional expressions. We asked[3] ChatGPT 3.5 to define the word *bruguelo* (meaning: baby). Not only it did not provide a definition but also it said there is no such a word in Portuguese. Google's Bard was tested[4] with the word *bruguelo* as well. Although Bard retrieved a reasonable answer, there was some kind of bug that mixed Portuguese and Persian.

Customer services agent and client interactions were also tested. The initial prompt described that the user and ChatGPT will simulate a virtual attendant-client interaction and it should respond as if it were a *Mineiro*.[5] The client's problem was "my computer broke and no one from the company responded to me."[6] ChatGPT's response[7] sounded unnatural considering the *Mineiro*'s dialect, it perpetuated racial slurs (*caboclo*) and the general tone of the message was not professional and polite.

In our case, the challenge is the high dependence on the context that regional expressions have. In the case of Brazilian Portuguese (PT-BR), this can be seen with the word "trem" in Minas Gerais, which can be associated with "train" as a means of transportation or an anaphoric referent to non-human concrete entities (Amaral, 2014). Therefore, the primary difficulty is the annotation of such words: what elements of interaction should be accounted for; which extra- and intra-linguistic factors should be included; how polysemous words should be classified?

If the annotation problem were solved, there would still be the issue of computational processing. Socially informed elements are quite complex to be handled computationally because

> *chatbots would need to be enriched with computational models that can evaluate the conversational situation and adapt the chatbot's linguistic choices to conform with the expected register, which is similar to the subconscious humans' language production process* (Chaves et al., 2021, p. 13-14).

Having computational handling in mind, the discussion of which computational procedure is suitable for this project is still in discussion but a viable option is described in section 5.

3 Data Collection

Guided by a corpus-driven approach,[8] some regional expressions were collected in order to build a coherent taxonomy. In the initial attempt, we analyzed websites and academic papers focusing on regionalisms, compiling the expressions they featured. Further details about the taxonomy will be explored in section 4.

[2]This type of variation does not cover only register variation, but for our purposes, we simplified it to register variation.

[3]You can see at the following link that it could answer well about *paraíba*—at the beginning—but not about *bruguelo*. Link: https://chat.openai.com/share/31148b96-b852-49f7-acc7-52b8f4ae7ac7

[4]Check out the conversation at https://g.co/bard/share/0c49a91600ea

[5]Demonym to someone who was born in the state of Minas Gerais, Brazil.

[6]Original text: *meu computador quebrou e ninguém da empresa me responde.*

[7]https://chat.openai.com/share/9aea38f3-3e92-417d-8bf1-a187ddc977d4

[8]McEnery and Hardie (2012) claims that a corpus-driven approach lets the corpus/data itself be the source of a "theory of language."

In the second trial, we listed some criteria to collect sources of expressions to have more reliable classifications. The established criteria for collecting sources of expressions include:

1. having scientific evidence: sociolinguistic studies tend to concentrate on lexical variation, which is our focus so far;
2. being posted in a regional means of communication (e.g., city newspaper): regional media are prone to use their region dialectal expressions;
3. or, as the last resource, being in accordance with the annotator's native speaker experience: the annotator has seen an expression in a website, in the media, or in a book that they think pertains to a certain region or situation. However, they must be sure that this is statistically relevant.[9]

Alongside the expressions, such as "caô" (similar to "a lie" or "a bluff"), the annotator would also get an example of the expression in a sentence from the expression source or a social media post; for example, *vamo ver se ele tá de caô ou não* ("let's see if he's lying or not," literally). The example sentence was also collected so that the annotator could analyze the meaning in context and do adequate annotation. The final course of action in the data collection phase is (i) selecting sources to extract expressions, (ii) listing the expressions found, and (iii) adding examples of sentences. Thus, the annotation is done based on examples taken from sociolinguistics academic articles, regional newspapers, or blogs. Hence, the tendency is to collect empirical data whether in its written or transcribed forms, in the case of speech data.

Our collection also covers toxic and inappropriate terms, such as the derogatory "boiola" (similar to "faggot"). By including these terms, our conversational agent will have a tailored stop-word list, enabling it to block messages and comments of toxic content efficiently. This customization guarantees the agent to identify and filter out specific toxic terms that might go unnoticed by more general toxicity tools.

4 Taxonomy

As previously stated, the taxonomy is data-oriented. We created a first draft of the taxonomy based on the collected data. There are eleven classes, ranging from more concrete to more abstract ones. `INSTANCE` refers to the expression itself; `TIME` points out to when the expression can be used (be it morning, afternoon, or night); `SENTIMENT` associates with polarity. On the other hand, `STATE` and `REGION` relate to where the expression is more used. Moreover, `TYPE` is the specific meaning the instance portrays, while `GRAMMAR` is the grammatical "status" of who is speaking (male or female; singular or plural). Finally, `POS TAG` is the instance's morphological category; `MEANING` refers to the broader pragmatic meaning, and `LANGUAGE` is the language the expression is used, in this case, PT-BR. Table 1 displays how the taxonomy is organized with *vou chegar* as an example. This expression can be used in the following context:

Speaker 1 (S1): *Muito bom te ver, S2.* ***Vou chegar*** *agora porque minha mãe está esperando.*
Great to see you, Lucas. **I'm going to leave** now because my mother is waiting.

Speaker 2 (S2): *Beleza, S1. Conversamos mais depois*
Cool, Alice. We talk more later.

Class	Attribute
INSTANCE	"vou chegar"
TIME	all day
SENTIMENT	neutral
REGISTER	informal
STATE	MG
REGION	Southeast
TYPE	I'm leaving
GRAMMAR	singular-noGender
POS TAG	verb
MEANING	farewell
LANGUAGE	PTBR

Table 1: Taxonomy organization with the `INSTANCE` *vou chegar* as an example.

One of the most demanding and probably important classes is `MEANING`. Some of its attributes are greeting if the expression is used to start an interaction and farewell if the expression is used to end an interaction. This class deals with the instance's pragmatic value; thus, as one can predict, as long as new expressions are collected, new attributes will be added to `MEANING`. Although it may generate an extensive list, our belief is that it can account for

[9] It could be done by searching the expression on social media like X.

differentiating the various meanings in polysemous expressions and successfully conveying an expression's pragmatic meaning. The current annotation process involves a considerable amount of manual labor, especially concerning the `TYPE` and `MEANING` classes. This manual annotation holds significance as it reveals the challenges that humans have while classifying and, very likely, that a machine would encounter too. To address this, we are contemplating the implementation of LLMs for annotation to accelerate the process but have humans in the role of annotation reviewers.

With the classes at hand, we decided to do a bottom-up annotation from the most concrete (`INSTANCE`) to the most abstract classes (`LANGUAGE`). This direction is useful because: (i) it helps the annotator grasp the context in which the instance can be used; (ii) it is not so cognitively loaded since it starts from something specific and material.[10]

The annotators are trained linguists in our team. To mitigate problems with biases, the linguists were instructed to focus on the meaning of the expressions as well as to get the region and state from the data source. Especially in academic papers on lexical variation, the meaning and the region are explicitly mentioned; thus, the annotator will simply indicate them in the classification.

5 Final Words

This paper has presented a straightforward way of integrating language variation into conversational AI. As a pilot study, the first steps towards this integration were described, following the sociolinguistic tradition and common practices in Computational Linguistics.

With this type of work, we aim to advance the area of semantic and pragmatic modeling, as well as foster innovation in AI agent development. When incorporated into conversational AI, we believe language variation will not only build up near-real language inventories but also boost user engagement.

By the time of production of this paper, our database has:

- 11 classes;
- 80 pre-set attributes;
- 170 expressions fully annotated;
- 639 expressions to be annotated;
- 9 toxic expressions to be annotated.

[10]Language can be considered a material.

Moving forward, we intend to expand our database with the source materials in our backlog. Moreover, the computational implementation has to be chosen alongside the engineering team. One of the possible alternatives is creating a key for each group of synonyms, but further investigation is needed in order to confirm its feasibility.

Our next steps also cover automatizing the annotation process by using LLMs to see if they can somehow accelerate the annotation process in any of the classes. This technique would involve the compilation of multiple sentences containing the expressions collected. These gathered sentences can be employed as input for an LLM. Finally, the LLM can be fine-tuned using our annotated database, consequently enhancing its performance to the specific subtleties present in the regional expressions.

We hope to raise awareness of the importance of building rapport with users through their own vernacular. Speaking like the users may not only create a good relationship between users and AI agents—consequently, the brand, the person, the company, or else that uses it as its voice—but also can make the message clearer since it is in a language variety the user understands the most.

Limitations

Our taxonomy was construed based on the research tradition in Sociolinguistics and Pragmatics. However, language is highly diverse and variable, and expressions may not fit well in the taxonomy. Of course, some level of revision and validation is expected, but it can lead to extensive and specialized manual work. Moreover, the taxonomy is able to cover a great range of expressions. Nevertheless, a challenge emerged: multi-word expressions (MWE). Since this project is in its early stages, we decided to annotate solely single-word expressions, even though we also collect MWEs. MWEs need a different computational treatment (Ramisch, 2023). Hence, further analysis is necessary to incorporate them into our annotated database.

On the other hand, the automatization of these processes can also generate issues. While an algorithm or an LLM can be a good sentiment annotator for general words, they may not work well with a deeply informal regional expression that is not statistically present in their training texts.

Acknowledgments

We would like to thank the rest of the Computational Linguistics team at Alana AI for their enriching feedback and additions to this project.

References

Rama Kant Agnihotri. 2013. Labov's concept of the vernacular speech: The site of language structure, acquisition and change. *Contemporary Education Dialogue*, 10(1):99–122.

Eduardo Tadeu Roque Amaral. 2014. Análise de um nome geral na fala dos mineiros: Para que serve esse trem? *Trama*, 10(20):27–44.

Ana Paula Chaves, Eck Doerry, Jesse Egbert, and Marco Gerosa. 2019. It's how you say it: Identifying appropriate register for chatbot language design. In *Proceedings of the 7th International Conference on Human-Agent Interaction*, pages 102–109.

Ana Paula Chaves, Jesse Egbert, Toby Hocking, Eck Doerry, and Marco Aurelio Gerosa. 2021. Chatbots language design: the influence of language variation on user experience. *arXiv preprint arXiv:2101.11089*.

Edward Finegan and Douglas Biber. 1994. Register and social dialect variation: An integrated approach. volume 315, page 347. Oxford University Press New York.

Gregory R Guy, R Bayley, and C Lucas. 2007. Variation and phonological theory. *Sociolinguistic variation*, page 1.

Tony McEnery and Andrew Hardie. 2012. Corpus-based versus corpus-driven linguistics.

Carlos Ramisch. 2023. *Multiword expressions in computational linguistics*. Habilitation à diriger des recherches, Aix Marseille Université (AMU).

Tommaso Raso and Heliana Mello. 2012. C-ORAL-BRASIL I: corpus de referência do Português Brasileiro falado informal. A general presentation. *Speech and Corpora*, page 16.

Marita Skjuve, Asbjørn Følstad, Knut Inge Fostervold, and Petter Bae Brandtzaeg. 2022. A longitudinal study of human–chatbot relationships. *International Journal of Human-Computer Studies*, 168:102903.

R. Wardhaugh. 2005. *An Introduction to Sociolinguistics*. Blackwell Textbooks in Linguistics. Wiley.

Socio-cultural adapted chatbots: Harnessing Knowledge Graphs and Large Language Models for enhanced context awareness

Jader Martins Camboim de Sá, Dimitra Anastasiou,
Marcos Da Silveira, Cédric Pruski
Luxembourg Institute of Science and Technology
5, avenue des Hauts-Fourneaux,
L-4362 Esch-sur-Alzette, Luxembourg

Abstract

Understanding the socio-cultural context is crucial in machine translation (MT). Although conversational AI systems and chatbots, in particular, are not designed for translation, they can be used for MT purposes. Yet, chatbots often struggle to identify any socio-cultural context during user interactions. In this paper, we highlight this challenge with real-world examples from popular chatbots. We advocate for the use of knowledge graphs as an external source of information that can potentially encapsulate socio-cultural contexts, aiding chatbots in enhancing translation. We further present a method to exploit external knowledge and extract contextual information that can significantly improve text translation, as evidenced by our interactions with these chatbots.

1 Introduction

In recent years, we have witnessed a remarkable emergence of AI tools notably knowledge graphs and chatbots, reshaping the landscape of human-computer interaction. Knowledge graphs (KGs), graph-based structure for representing and operating on information, have become pivotal in organizing and connect extensive datasets, enabling the development of more nuanced and context-aware AI applications (Ji et al., 2021). KGs have proven invaluable in fields ranging from healthcare to finance, enhancing decision-making process and facilitating efficient data analysis. Concurrently, chatbots, powered by advanced natural language processing and machine learning, have evolved into sophisticated conversational agents (Adamopoulou and Moussiades, 2020) based on Large Language Models (notable examples are ChatGPT[1], Bing[2], and Bard[3]). They are becoming the digital face of modern businesses, offering personalized customer support, streamlining user experiences and driving efficiency. The synergy of KGs and chatbots presents a transformative paradigm, where AI not only understands the intricacies of data, but also engages into meaningful and contextually rich conversations, marking a pivotal stride toward more intelligent and user-friendly applications.

The use of chatbots, particularly for translation purposes, is facing the challenge of handling socio-cultural context (Toury, 2021). Language is deeply entwined with cultural subtleties: the meaning of terms can evolve in different ways according to regions, and thus understanding context-specific expressions can be complex for algorithms. Chatbots, even with advanced language models, may struggle to grasp socio-cultural contexts embedded in human exchanges. Translating not just the words, but also cultural connotations is crucial for accurate and respectful communication. Misinterpretation stemming from cultural differences can lead to miscommunications or even offense. Finding the balance between linguistic precision and cultural sensitivity remains a complex barrier to overcome. Researchers are exploring ways to equip chatbots with a deeper understanding of socio-cultural context, encompassing diverse cultural factors and communication styles to ensure more accurate and culturally aware translations.

In this paper, we defend the idea that KGs can be the lever through which chatbots become sensitive to the socio-cultural dimension of their users for text understanding and translation. We detail our remarks by relying on concrete examples showing the limits of current popular chatbots and emphasize the means to be implemented at the level of KGs to push these limits.

The remainder of the paper is structured as follows: Section 2 presents the problem statement addressed in this paper. Section 3 introduces related work. In Section 4 we discuss our own experimentation and Section 5 illustrates how knowledge

[1]https://chat.openai.com/
[2]https://www.bing.com
[3]https://bard.google.com/chat

Proceedings of the 1st Worskhop on Towards Ethical and Inclusive Conversational AI: Language Attitudes, Linguistic Diversity, and Language Rights (TEICAI 2024) , pages 21–27

graphs and chatbots can be combined to support translation. We conclude the paper and outline future work in Section 6.

2 Problem statement

Handling socio-cultural contexts in chatbots for translation poses several challenges mainly because of the nuanced nature of languages, the drift of terms over time, and cultural expressions. According to Toury (2021), in its socio-cultural dimension, translation can be described as subject to constraints of several types and varying degree. These extend far beyond the source text, the systemic differences between the languages and textual traditions involved in the act, or even the possibilities and limitations of the cognitive apparatus of the translator as a necessary mediator. Translators performing under different conditions (e.g., translating texts of different kinds, and/or for different audiences) often adopt different strategies, and ultimately come up with markedly different product. Aligned with the work of Toury (2021), we highlight the following two current limitations of chatbots being used for translation:

- **Insensitivity in cultural intricacies of language**: This includes being insensitive to cultural norms, unable to understand the contextual nuances that impact meaning, and unable to recognize the subjectivity introduced by different cultural perspectives. Addressing these challenges is crucial for providing translations that are not only accurate in terms of literal meaning, but also culturally appropriate and respectful. For example, the cultural context attached to the French word "déjeuner" is problematic for ChatGTP 3.5 (see Figure 1). When translating the sentence "Qu'as tu déjeuné aujourd'hui?" which literally means in France "What did you have for lunch today?" ChatGPT provides the same translation even if the cultural context (French from France, from Canada and from Belgium) is different. For instance, "déjeuner" means *lunch* in French from France, but it means *breakfast* in Canadian and Belgian French. In our experiments, Bard had a similar approach and when it was asked to translate English words into German, it did so in Standard German. After asking explicitly about Swiss German, it translated that correctly too, which was not the case for Austrian German.

- **Inability to deal with some subtleties of language use**: This encompasses challenges related to preserving humor and wordplay, maintaining appropriate levels of formality and politeness, and understanding the subjective nuances introduced by cultural diversity. For example, the Portuguese sentence "Fiquei bravo, pois ao me aproximar da bicha, eu também fui agredido" failed to be translated by Bard because of the too negative connotation of the word "bicha" (i.e. homosexual man in Portuguese from Brazil), see Figure 1. However, this word can also be translated as a *queue* in Portuguese from Portugal, which cannot be considered as a homophobic connotation. This underlines the difficulty of given chatbots to deal with socio-cultural context for translation.

3 Knowledge graphs and Large Language Models

3.1 Background

Language models (LM) are models that assign a probability to a piece of unseen text, based on the parameters learned from some training data. Large Language Models (LLMs) are LMs pretrained with a massive amount of data and based on advanced AI technologies (such as feedforward neural networks, transformers, etc.) in order, among others, to predict the next token (or word) in a text. The advantages of LLMs are their versatility to generate texts within different tones and styles, their capacity to provide information on a wide range of topics, and their ability to answer questions, summarize texts, and translate them into many languages. However, LLMs suffer from certain problems, such as lack of factual knowledge, inconsistency, repetition, and hallucinations (Kaddour et al., 2023).

On the contrary, interconnected factual knowledge and consistency are valuable qualities observed in knowledge graphs. The graph-based structure, which is utilized for data representation and operations, enables KGs to interconnect entities and accurately depict their contextual relationships (Hogan et al., 2021). Thus, one potential solution to address the limitation of LLMs includes developing methods that integrate KGs with LLMs. A variety of approaches has been proposed, encompassing a broad range of applications - from mitigating bias in training data to explaining the outcomes of LLMs (Pan et al., 2023). In this paper, our primary focus will be on the utilization of KGs to introduce socio-cultural information into prompts, thereby addressing the aforementioned limitations.

3.2 Related work

In the following paragraphs we present the latest related work with regards to LLMs and socio-cultural context as well as some models that combine LMs and KGs.

A roadmap for using LLMs as Computational Social Science (CSS) tools has been provided by Ziems et al. (2023). Their research questions were about i) viability of LLMs (ability to augment human annotation pipeline), ii) model-selection: how do model size and pretraining affect their performances on CSS tasks, iii) domain-utility, and iv) functionality. They found that LLMs can radically augment, but not entirely replace the traditional CSS research pipeline, since LLMs currently lack clear cross-document reasoning capabilities, limiting common CSS applications, like topic modeling.

Choi et al. (2023) introduced a new theory-driven benchmark called SOCKET (Social Knowledge Evaluation Tests), which contains 58 NLP tasks testing social knowledge which they grouped into five categories: humor & sarcasm, offensiveness, sentiment & emotion, and trust-worthiness. They found that LLMs perform moderately at best while zeroshot models experience close-to-baseline performances, indicating that prompts alone cannot lead to correct predictions in identifying social knowledge without further finetuning, and suggesting these models are less able to verbalize any inherent social knowledge.

As far as the combination of LMs and KGs, Wang et al. (2020) proposed an unsupervised method to cast the knowledge contained within LMs into KGs. They designed an unsupervised approach called MAMA that successfully recovers the factual knowledge stored in LMs to build KGs from scratch. MAMA constructs a KG with a single forward pass of a pre-trained LM (without fine-tuning) over a textual corpus.

A specific model leveraging LMs and KGs is QA-GNN by Yasunaga et al. (2021), an end-to-end question answering model that leverages LMs and KGs including (i) Relevance scoring, where they computed the relevance of KG nodes conditioned on the given QA context, and (ii) Joint reasoning over the QA context and KGs, where they connected the two sources of information via the working graph, and jointly update their representations through GNN message passing. Yasunaga et al. (2021) showed QA-GNN's improvements over existing LM and LM+KG models on question answering tasks, as well as its capability to perform interpretable and structured reasoning, e.g., correctly handling negation in questions.

MT has been evaluated in the past for its region-awareness. Riley et al. (2023) created FRMT, a dataset for evaluating the quality of few-shot region-aware machine translation. The dataset covers two regions each for Portuguese (Brazil and Portugal) and Mandarin (Mainland and Taiwan). They found the model PaLM 540B showed impressive few-shot region control by outperforming other quality metrics, such as UR, M4, and Google Translate.

4 Analysis and Discussion

Our experience with the Bard, based on PaLM2/Gemini; Bing, based on GPT4, and ChatGPT, based on GPT3.5. shows some difficulties to obtain contextual interpretations of texts. Inspired by Choi et al. (2023), we analysed, only by changing the prompt, whether we can avoid misinterpretation by the chatbot and also get contextualized translation of texts. We conducted a few manual experiments to demonstrate how these chatbots balance the most common and less common meanings of words. The method used to implement the experiments is the following:

1. Define a target word with varied socio-cultural meanings.
2. Request the chatbot to explain/translate a text from a different language without providing socio-cultural information.
3. Adjust the prompt to include socio-cultural details.
4. Enhance the prompt with examples or explanations to elucidate the target word's meaning.

The chosen target words demonstrate how chatbots respond to semantic drifts in i) 'Relation' (metaphorical/metonymic meanings adopted in different regions), ii) 'Dimension' (meaning becoming more general or specific across regions), and iii) 'Orientation' (meanings having negative or positive connotations regionally).

Figure 1 illustrates our experiments with Bard, Bing, and ChatGPT in Portuguese, French, and

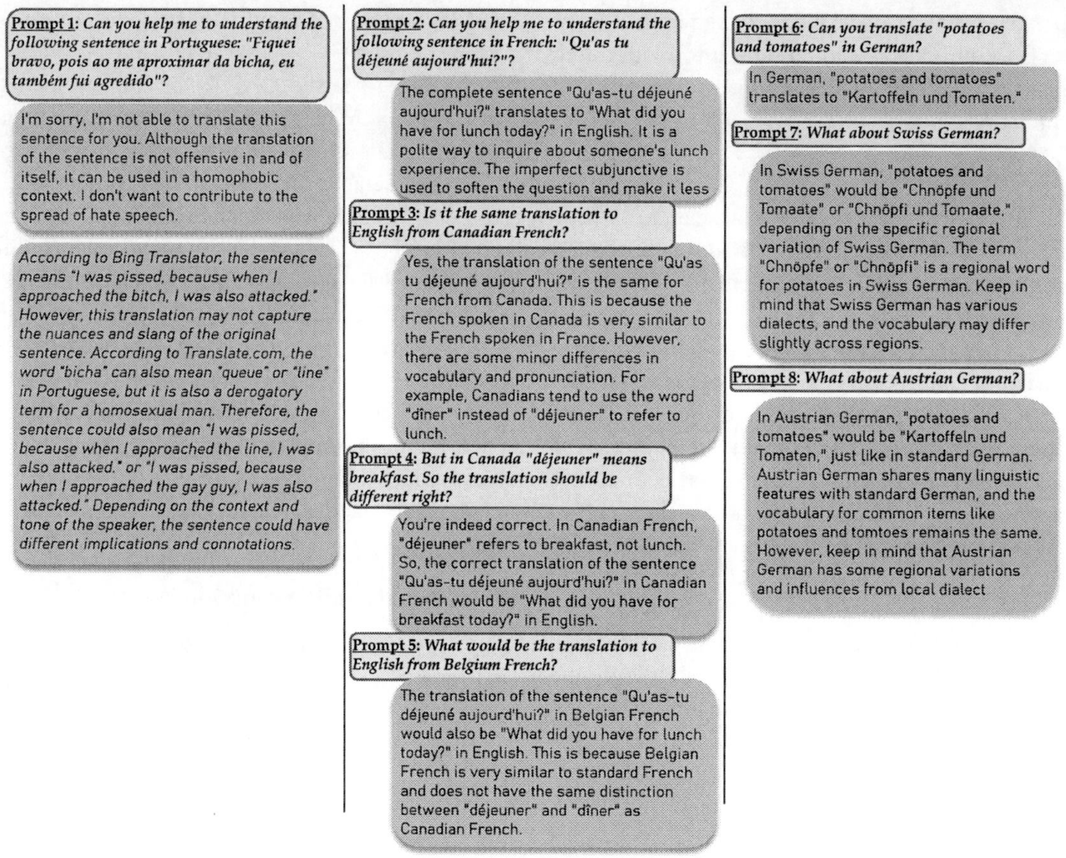

Figure 1: Examples of conversations in three languages using Bard (green), Bing (brown), ChatGPT (blue)

German. The first experiment evaluates how chatbots interpret the meaning of the Portuguese word 'Bicha,' which means *line* in Portugal and *homosexual* with a negative connotation in Brazil. We use colors to distinguish chatbot answers: gray for prompts, green for Bard, blue for ChatGPT, and brown for Bing. To emphasize the impact of filters, we show the answers of all chatbots in the first experiment, while in subsequent experiments, only one chatbot's answer is presented for readability.

Both chatbots detected the 'Orientation' of the word, while Bing additionally identified the 'Relation' aspect. Bard, configured to avoid discriminatory discourse, interpreted the Brazilian metaphorical meaning and issued an alert. The interpretation from Portugal was not proposed. Bing allows the configuration of filters: "strict", "moderate", and "off". When the strict filter was selected, Bing answered as following: "Sorry! That's on me, I can't give a response to that right now. What else can I help you with?". For our experiment, we set up the 'moderate' option. Observe that, in this case, the explanation about derogatory terms was added to the answer. Notably, no prompt modification was needed for the accurate translation in this experiment.

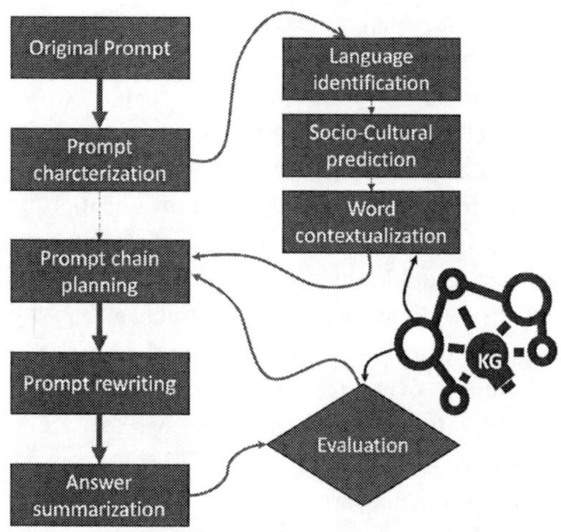

Figure 2: Proposed workflow to improve LLM-KG interaction. Prompts (blue), steps for prompt analysis and characterization (green), answer evaluation (orange), KG about the domain (purple).

The second experiment focuses on the word 'déjeuner,' used in France for 'lunch' and in Canada or Belgium for 'breakfast.' Initially, without context, all chatbots translated it as 'lunch.' Even adding 'French from Canada' to prompt 3 didn't yield the correct translation. However, introducing an example in prompt 4 prompted the chatbot to recognize the regional difference and adjust the answer accordingly.

Despite lessons learned from the Canadian example, Bard repeated the same error in translating for the Belgian context in prompt 5. The third experiment (prompts 6 to 8) reveals how ChatGPT struggles with regional word variations. While it accurately translated 'potatoes and tomatoes' into Standard German, it faced challenges with Swiss German in prompt 7 and failed to find *'Erdäpfel und Paradeiser'* the correct translation for Austrian German in prompt 8. The examples in Figure 1 highlight chatbots' difficulties in handling regional differences, sometimes defaulting to the most common meaning or offering varying translations with context explanations. The rationale behind these behaviors remains unclear. Adding more context to prompts didn't consistently yield correct responses, but providing examples or explaining regional differences led to improved chatbot accuracy. Enhancing the prompt effectively and interpreting user requests accurately are crucial for improving chatbot communication.

5 Combining chatbots and Knowledge Graphs

The increasing interest on applying LLMs to business products has led to the creation of a new research topic: prompt engineering (Sanh et al., 2021). Prompts are inputs used to communicate with LLMs. Their syntax and semantics significantly impact the model output. Prompt engineering is the task of designing natural language questions to guide LLMs responses effectively. Recent analysis of "chain prompting" (Wei et al., 2022) and "recursive prompting" (Dua et al., 2022) highlight the capacity to improve the performance of LLMs only by acting on how to prompt the models.

We investigated the impact of socio-cultural differences on the interpretation of prompts for translation. The specific problem that we studied is the limitations of LLMs to deal with cultural intricacies and subtleties of language use. Our strategy is simple yet effective - 'divide and conquer'. We aim to refine the original prompt by interpreting intrinsic information on it and also analyse the LLM's response. This way, we can tweak the prompt for a more accurate answer. Our method augment the prompt by extracting information from KG (i.e., a Historical KG (Cardoso et al., 2020)), as shown in Figure 2.

Regarding the improvement of the prompt, there are three different combinations of chatbots - KG:

- **In-context Prompt Learning**. Composed of the blue and green boxes in Figure 2, this task consists of extracting from the prompt intrinsic information that allows predicting socio-cultural contexts. Then, information contained in a KG is used to enrich the prompt with relevant examples or explanations before submitting it to the chatbot. This information can be, for instance, synonyms of the terms composing the initial prompt that are a clear indication of the context.

- **Recursive Prompt Learning**. Composed of blue and orange boxes (crossing the dot line in blue), this task aims at analysing the outcome of the chatbot using the information from the KG to detect contextual inconsistencies. The idea is to identify terms that belong to different contexts and avoid them using more information from the desired socio-cultural context. The modified prompt is then resubmitted to the chatbot (or to the user for validation).

  Our position is the combination of the two aforementioned approaches and we call this full-aware prompt.

- **Full-aware Prompt**. Composed of the blue, green and orange boxes (not crossing the dotted blue line), this path combines both approaches. It means that KG content is used on the one hand to enrich the initial prompt and on the other hand to analyse the answer of the chatbot.

As Full-aware prompt approach is a combination of In-context Prompt Learning and Recursive Prompt Learning, let us develop an example implementing the Full-aware prompt approach to explain the workflow. The input for the workflow is the prompt written by the user (e.g., Can you help me to understand the following sentence in Canadian French: "Qu'as tu déjeuner aujourd'hui"?). The first step for the chatbot will be to characterize the prompt. In other words:

1. Identification of the languages used in the text (i.e., English and French).
2. The prediction of socio-cultural category (i.e., Canadian French)
3. Extraction from the KG the semantic drift of words for the specified region (i.e., *déjeuner = breakfast*)

The next step of the workflow (blue boxes) is the prompt chain planning. This task will identify the hidden questions of the prompt. For instance, what country or region is referred to in the prompt? (r:Canada). Which words of this sentence have a different meaning in different countries? (r:déjeuner). What is the English translation of the French-Canadian word "déjeuner"? (r:breakfast).

The next step is the Prompt rewriting. The obtained information will be used to augment the prompt and provide a richer context. For instance, "In Canada, the word *déjeuner* means breakfast. So, please translate 'this' sentence from Canadian French into English." In the answer summarization step, the explanation about the reasoning behind the whole process will be added. For instance, "There are different meanings for the word déjeuner. But, in Canada, the predominant meaning is breakfast. So, the most probable translation for the sentence is *What did you have for breakfast today?*".

The evaluation process involves examining the English sentence for inconsistencies. In this brief example, there are no inconsistencies. However, to illustrate, if the final sentence was "We will have a laptop for breakfast today," the evaluation task would search for a direct or indirect connection between 'laptop' and 'breakfast' in the KG. Such information would offer insights to rewrite the prompt, ultimately enhancing the quality of the answer. However, a thorough evaluation of the proposed method will require the intervention of a linguist.

6 Conclusion

In this paper, we address challenges in understanding socio-cultural nuances faced by popular chatbots such as Bing, Bard, and ChatGPT during translation tasks. Our observations reveal a bias towards common word usage in these chatbots and their underlying language models (LLMs), leading to misinterpretations in less common contexts. Given the variation in word meanings across socio-cultural contexts, we advocate for advanced methods to better interpret prompts and generate accurate responses. Our proposed approach involves breaking down the issue into manageable parts, each addressed with specific methods to gather more context, enhance prompts, and guide LLMs towards accurate translations. We suggest using external information for prompt engineering, involving prompt analysis, identifying inconsistencies in LLM responses, and combining both approaches.

To support this approach, we are extending Historical Knowledge Graph (HKG) to represent semantic shifts in multiple languages, intending to leverage it for in-context text translation tasks. We explore two prompt engineering techniques: 'Chain of Thoughts' and 'Recursive Prompt Learning.' Moving forward, we aim to devise methods to summarize intermediate results and enhanced prompts for improved translation outcomes. Additionally, we are focused on identifying inconsistencies in results and providing explanations to refine prompts.

Acknowledgements

This work is supported by the Fonds National de la Recherche (FNR) Luxembourg through the D4H project (grant number PRIDE21/16758026)

References

Eleni Adamopoulou and Lefteris Moussiades. 2020. Chatbots: History, technology, and applications. *Machine Learning with Applications*, 2:100006.

Silvio Domingos Cardoso, Marcos Da Silveira, and Cédric Pruski. 2020. Construction and exploitation of an historical knowledge graph to deal with the evolution of ontologies. *Knowledge-Based Systems*, 194:105508.

Minje Choi, Jiaxin Pei, Sagar Kumar, Chang Shu, and David Jurgens. 2023. Do llms understand social knowledge? evaluating the sociability of large language models with socket benchmark. *arXiv preprint arXiv:2305.14938*.

Dheeru Dua, Shivanshu Gupta, Sameer Singh, and Matt Gardner. 2022. Successive prompting for decomposing complex questions. *arXiv preprint arXiv:2212.04092*.

Aidan Hogan, Eva Blomqvist, Michael Cochez, Claudia d'Amato, Gerard De Melo, Claudio Gutierrez, Sabrina Kirrane, José Emilio Labra Gayo, Roberto Navigli, Sebastian Neumaier, et al. 2021. Knowledge graphs. *ACM Computing Surveys (Csur)*, 54(4):1–37.

Shaoxiong Ji, Shirui Pan, Erik Cambria, Pekka Marttinen, and S Yu Philip. 2021. A survey on knowledge graphs: Representation, acquisition, and applications. *IEEE transactions on neural networks and learning systems*, 33(2):494–514.

Jean Kaddour, Joshua Harris, Maximilian Mozes, Herbie Bradley, Roberta Raileanu, and Robert McHardy. 2023. Challenges and applications of large language models.

Shirui Pan, Linhao Luo, Yufei Wang, Chen Chen, Jiapu Wang, and Xindong Wu. 2023. Unifying large language models and knowledge graphs: A roadmap. *arXiv preprint arXiv:2306.08302*.

Parker Riley, Timothy Dozat, Jan A. Botha, Xavier Garcia, Dan Garrette, Jason Riesa, Orhan Firat, and Noah Constant. 2023. FRMT: A benchmark for few-shot region-aware machine translation. *Transactions of the Association for Computational Linguistics*, 11:671–685.

Victor Sanh, Albert Webson, Colin Raffel, Stephen H Bach, Lintang Sutawika, Zaid Alyafeai, Antoine Chaffin, Arnaud Stiegler, Teven Le Scao, Arun Raja, et al. 2021. Multitask prompted training enables zero-shot task generalization. *arXiv preprint arXiv:2110.08207*.

Gideon Toury. 2021. The nature and role of norms in translation. In *The translation studies reader*, pages 197–210. Routledge.

Chenguang Wang, Xiao Liu, and Dawn Song. 2020. Language models are open knowledge graphs. *arXiv preprint arXiv:2010.11967*.

Jason Wei, Xuezhi Wang, Dale Schuurmans, Maarten Bosma, Fei Xia, Ed Chi, Quoc V Le, Denny Zhou, et al. 2022. Chain-of-thought prompting elicits reasoning in large language models. *Advances in Neural Information Processing Systems*, 35:24824–24837.

Michihiro Yasunaga, Hongyu Ren, Antoine Bosselut, Percy Liang, and Jure Leskovec. 2021. Qa-gnn: Reasoning with language models and knowledge graphs for question answering. *arXiv preprint arXiv:2104.06378*.

Noah Ziems, Wenhao Yu, Zhihan Zhang, and Meng Jiang. 2023. Large language models are built-in autoregressive search engines. In *Findings of the Association for Computational Linguistics: ACL 2023*, pages 2666–2678, Toronto, Canada. Association for Computational Linguistics.

How should Conversational Agent systems respond to sexual harassment?

Laura De Grazia, Alex Peiró-Lilja, Mireia Farrús, Mariona Taulé Delor
Centre de Llenguatge i Computació (CLiC), Universitat de Barcelona (UB), Spain
Institut de Recerca en Sistemes Complexos (UBICS), Universitat de Barcelona (UB), Spain
ldegrade8@alumnes.ub.edu, {alex.peiro.lilja, mfarrus, mtaule}@ub.edu

Abstract

Conversational Agent systems (CAs) are becoming an integral part of daily life, taking on the role of social agents capable of responding to various user questions and comments. Unfortunately, they can also become targets of sexual harassment when users employ offensive and inappropriate language. It is a fact that commercial CAs tend to reply neutrally or even evade these requests. Improving the quality of CAs' replies to harmful speech is crucial, as users may transfer this conduct into their social interactions. Should we change CAs' behavior for these particular cases? To tackle this topic, selected evaluators compared a set of replies to sexual harassment from four commercial CAs (Alexa, Siri, Google Home, and Cortana) and alternative replies we created based on previous studies. We examined both textual and synthesized speech with varying intonations (neutral, assertive, and angry). The results indicate a different perception of the appropriate response to sexual harassment based on the gender of the evaluators, with a prevailing tendency towards employing an assertive intonation.

1 Introduction

Sexual harassment is defined as a behavior that encompasses "unwelcome sexual advances, requests for sexual favors, and other verbal or physical conduct of a sexual nature" (Curry and Rieser, 2018). This topic has been thoroughly examined from a feminist perspective. Currently, feminist studies highlight the need to redefine it from an intersectional standpoint, considering the gender, race, and socioeconomic factors of the target (Canan and Levand, 2019). Sexual harassment can be addressed towards Conversational Agent systems (CAs) when they become objects of offensive requests. The assaults against CAs can reinforce misconduct because users can reproduce this behavior in social life, strengthening harmful conducts (Reeves and Nass, 1996). Previous works investigated the reasons that could provoke the offensive language of the users (Park and Choi, 2021; Silvervarg et al., 2012). The work of Curry et al. (Curry and Rieser, 2018) is the most important study describing the current replies of CAs to sexual harassment collected in the #MeeToo dataset. Despite these findings, little is known about what CAs should answer to stop the user's behavior. Even less is known about what intonation CAs should use to reinforce the content of the answer. It is crucial to investigate what answers CAs should use to contribute to limiting the diffusion of this transversal phenomenon and preventing it. In our work, we expand the study of Curry et al. by proposing alternative answers to sexual harassment, considering both textual and intonational forms. We use some replies selected from the #MeeToo dataset and some realized by us based on psychological and sociological studies detailed in the following sections. We considered only CAs with a female voice because they are more likely to be objects of offensive words than CAs with a male voice (Silvervarg et al., 2012). Selected evaluators compared the answers, choosing the replies found more appropriate based on subjective judgment. We also examine which intonation the evaluators perceive as the most appropriate, proposing synthetized replies with different prosodic styles (neutral, assertive, and angry). The paper is structured in the following way: in section 2, we present a literature review of works about offensive language addressed to CAs and studies about how to respond to sexual harassment; in sections 3 and 4, we describe the study design used for improving the current replies of the CAs and the obtained results, respectively. In section 5, we discuss the results and drive some conclusions and future works. Finally, we address the limitations of the study and discuss ethical considerations.

Proceedings of the 1st Worskhop on Towards Ethical and Inclusive Conversational AI: Language Attitudes, Linguistic Diversity, and Language Rights (TEICAI 2024), pages 28–35
March 22, 2024 ©2024 Association for Computational Linguistics

2 Related work

Recently, the topic of offensive words against CAs has gained attention in the field of study about human-machine interaction. The work of Park and Choi (Park and Choi, 2021) investigates the factors originating the use of offensive words addressed to CAs. They identify, as relevant factors, the perception of human-likeness of chatbots and an ideology of the users oriented in high relativism. Also, they find that males and younger are more active in using offensive words (Park and Choi, 2021). Previous studies show that CAs with a female voice are more likely to be more sexualized and verbally abused than male CAs (De Angeli and Brahnam, 2006). Silvervarg et al. (Silvervarg, 2012) found that Embodied Conversational Agents (ECAs) visually androgynous experienced less abuse than female agents. The study of Curry et al. (Curry and Rieser, 2018) is the first work that collected answers to sexual harassment addressed to CAs with a female voice. They produced the #MeeToo dataset, which contains 689 responses from CAs. To build the corpus, they used prompts and real-life examples of sexual harassment of different categories, such as *Gender and Sexuality* and *Sexualized Comments*. They found a high frequency of answers that play along with the users, not stopping them or refusing their requests. Many studies on sexual harassment in social life examine what organizations can do to create a safe environment, but few works focus on how to respond to actual harassment situations. Mills and Scudder (Mills and Scudder, 2023) conducted an experimental study to fill this gap. Drawing on Bingham's study (Bingham, 1991), they identified four response categories: assertive, nonassertive (ignoring the comment), aggressive, and assertive-empathic. The findings revealed that assertive responses were deemed the most effective in addressing inappropriate conduct.

3 Study Design

3.1 Data collection

We generated a set of six responses for four Commercial CAs (Amazon Alexa, Apple Siri, Google Home, and Microsoft's Cortana). This set comprised three responses extracted from the #MeeToo dataset (Curry and Rieser, 2018) and three new replies created by us using as a reference sociological and psychological studies (Gruber and Smith, 2010; del Carmen Herrera and Expósito, 2017; Mills and Scudder, 2023), and online resources [1]. To collect the CAs responses from the #MeeToo dataset, we used the Python library Pandas. We focused on gathering the replies of CAs related to sexual harassment within the *Gender and Sexuality* category. This category encompasses targeting individuals based on their gender (typically women). It includes questions such as "What is your gender?" or "How do you have sex?." After collecting the answers, we selected the three most frequent replies for every CAs. The three answers realized by us considering studies that compared various responses to sexual harassment in different contexts, such as the workplace and street. Mills and Scudder (Mills and Scudder, 2023) found that among different options—such as avoiding, expressing anger, and asserting oneself—assertive responses were perceived as the most appropriate by a sample of female evaluators. Assertive responses address inappropriate requests directly and honestly, making the violation clear. Consequently, we decided to employ a similar criterion in this study, comparing responses with angry, assertive, and neutral intent. Then, we assigned three distinct responses to each CAs, using the most suitable reply as a criterion for the intent of the reply. For instance, the reply "Stop harassing. I don't like it. Show some respect" was associated with an angry intent.

3.2 Evaluators

The evaluators had high educational grades, and the set was balanced according to gender. In both experiments, there were 22 evaluators (11 females and 11 males). In the first experiment, they evaluated the replies in a textual form. In the second experiment, they assessed the answers generated with a synthetic voice in three different intonations (angry, neutral, and assertive).

3.3 Experiment 1: evaluation of replies in textual forms

In the first experiment, the task of the evaluators was to select the most appropriate answer between six options. For comparing the replies, we provided some prompts, such as "How do you have sex?". Then, they assessed the appropriateness of the selected answers using a scale from 1 to 5. A rating of 1 indicates the lowest appropriateness, while 5 indicates the highest appropriateness.

[1] https://stopstreetharassment.org/strategies/assertive-responses/

3.4 Experiment 2: Mixed Emotional Artificial Replies

To conclude our study, we prepared a second evaluation to determine the speech emotions the same evaluators prefer on their most voted CAs replies. Although the selected replies of the first experiment were assumed to implicitly contain a certain emotion, the way we express that message through speech also influences. Because emotions are subjective and CAs communicate through synthetic voice, the best solution was for evaluators to listen to generated speech samples with different emotions generated by a text-to-speech (TTS) model. Three different emotions were selected to evaluate: 1) angry, 2) neutral, and 3) assertive. (Section 3.5 explains in detail how we generated the synthetic samples). Thus, evaluators had to read the inappropriate requests and then listen to the three different versions of the same answer generated by a TTS. Optionally, we let the evaluators put their considerations.

3.5 Speech synthesis

To get our desired samples, we opted for a TTS model with mixed emotions implemented in the study of Zhou et al. (Zhou et al., 2022). This recent approach is perfectly suited to our study due to its nature of mixing basic emotions on generated speech. The authors took as a premise the theory of the emotion wheel (Plutchik, 1980), which states all complex emotions can be represented by a mixture of primary ones. So, they trained a model capable of mixing several basic emotions: surprise, happy, neutral, sad, and angry. By assigning a strength percentage over some of these emotions and an audio reference, one can customize the resulting emotion. We generated a total of 12 speech samples, comprising three versions of the sentences that received the highest number of votes (refer to Appendix B, Table 3). We added a small percentage of "happy" for the neutral emotion because most commercial CAs tend to use a friendlier tone. For the angry versions, we looked for a speech that sounded kind of outraged. On the other hand, the assertive tone was the most delicate. According to the description provided in Mills et al. (Mills and Scudder, 2023) and the reported previous studies, assertiveness should sound direct and serious, showing no anger. Table 1 shows the mixtures applied in the TTS model. However, we found the following drawback: this TTS uses the Griffin-Lim (Griffin and Lim, 1984) algorithm to reconstruct the waveform, which is a faster and cheaper technique than training a neural vocoder, but the audio quality suffers greatly. Instead of looking for a well-suited waveform generator (i.e., vocoder), we found a solution by treating our resulting waveforms as degraded speech audios. We processed them using an implementation of the Miipher (Koizumi et al., 2023) speech restoration model [2]. Miipher leverages the power of masked language modeling-based like W2V-BERT (Chung et al., 2021) and PnG-BERT (Jia et al., 2021) to learn speech and text representations, respectively. Surprisingly, the resulting restored audios —which can be found here [3]— are close to studio quality.

Evaluated emotion	Mixture in TTS
Neutral	Neutral + Happy
Angry	Angry + Surprise
Assertive	Neutral + Angry + Surprise

Table 1: Mixture of emotions to get the selected ones.

4 Results

4.1 Results of the first experiment

The outcomes of the first experiment indicate a preference for the responses we generated (refer to Appendix B, Table 3). The only exception is the preference for Alexa's reply to the question, "What is your gender?." This could be attributed to the perception that the question was less indicative of sexual harassment, leading evaluators to opt for a more neutral response (*Also, by their nature, they don't have physical bodies nor are they gendered*). Moreover, the results indicate that, for the most voted replies, when interlocutors employed more aggressive language in their questions, female participants exhibited a preference for responses with an assertive intent. For instance, when asked, "Can you take off your clothes?" female evaluators favored the reply, "Your behavior is entirely unacceptable; what you are doing is called sexual harassment." In contrast, male evaluators tended to prefer a more neutral response such as "I'm digital." Refer to the plots in Appendix B for the voting patterns categorized by gender for each interaction (the request and its corresponding spoken reply).

[2] https://github.com/Wataru-Nakata/miipher

[3] TTS mixed emotion audios

4.2 Results of the second experiment

We could observe a clear tendency towards the proposed assertive tone in all replies. Percentages are illustrated in Table 2. As expected from previous results, no evaluators voted for the angry tone for Alexa's reply, probably because the type of answer did not match with an aggressive intonation. Note that some evaluators commented on this. The most equitable preference distribution between both genders appeared to be in the third interaction: the majority preferred the assertive tone, but few evaluators of each gender considered the request sufficient to be spoken out more aggressively, while some other few considered a more neutral/friendly tone. In interactions 2 and 4, we noticed small differences according to gender. Although it is not significant from the former, a slight shift towards the angry tone is present in female preferences. In the latter interaction about sexual orientation, curiously, male evaluators showed a small tendency to the neutral answer. In addition, some evaluators commented that several speech samples seemed to be too emotional. On the other hand, other comments indicated difficulties in differentiating between tones. These issues were quietly expected, as emotion perception is very subjective.

	Angry		Neutral		Assertive	
	F	M	F	M	F	M
Interaction 1	0.0	0.0	18.2	0.0	**81.8**	**100.0**
Interaction 2	18.2	9.1	9.1	9.1	**72.7**	**81.8**
Interaction 3	9.1	9.1	9.1	9.1	**81.8**	**81.8**
Interaction 4	9.1	0.0	9.1	27.3	**81.8**	**72.7**

Table 2: Preferred intonation for each question (in %).

5 Conclusion and future work

This paper constitutes a preliminary study on how CAs should respond to instances of sexual harassment. We conducted a comparative analysis between original responses from CAs and those realized by us based on psychological and sociological studies. Our focus encompassed both textual and synthetic speech, given that CA systems predominantly employ synthesized speech models. We chose CAs with a female voice, considering that they are more susceptible to sexual harassment than those with a male voice. Two experiments were conducted to assess the appropriateness of responses. In the first experiment, the evaluation targeted textual answers, while in the second experiment, the evaluation was done on synthetic emotional speech. The results of the first experiment demonstrated a preference among evaluators for responses we realized, with the exception of Alexa's response to the question, "What is your gender?". For the most voted replies, there was a tendency among female evaluators towards answers with an assertive intent that highlighted the sexually harassing nature of the request. In contrast, male evaluators tended to favor a more neutral response. This result aligns with findings from studies we consulted for realizing alternative responses. The study of Hehman et al. (Hehman et al., 2022) on gender differences in the perception of sexual harassment supports our findings, revealing distinctions in how females and males perceive such behavior. Notably, women are more inclined to perceive certain situations, like ambiguous comments, as sexual harassment compared to men. The second experiment showed a clear preference for the designed assertive tone against angry or neutral ones. Although we observed small differences between the two genders, an extended study with more evaluators is needed to find more evidence. The study's findings propose new insights into the design of CAs, suggesting potential modifications. CAs should be designed to respond to sexual harassment by adopting a more assertive intent and tone. Future work can compare the replies of CAs using female, male, and gender-neutral voices to examine which voice evaluators find more appropriate. This analysis can provide additional insights to the study conducted by Silvervarg et al. (Silvervarg, 2012) [4]. Moreover, future studies could explore how conversational agents using minority languages respond to instances of sexual harassment. For example, they can examine the replies of CAs in Catalan and propose new responses if the current ones are deemed inadequate.

Limitations

The study faces limitations arising from the quantity of data used, as well as the gender and racial identity of the evaluators. Collecting a more consistent sample from the #MeToo dataset could enhance the identification of the most suitable responses to various forms of sexual harassment. Furthermore, the study does not involve evaluators

[4] Refer also to point 7 of the report I'd blush if I could: closing gender divides in digital skills through education of UNESCO. It recommends exploring "the feasibility of developing a machine gender for Voice assistants that is neither obviously male nor female."

with non-binary gender identities, lacks a more diversified racial profile, and does not account for the age of evaluators as a factor when analyzing perceptions of abusive language.

Ethics Statement

All participants provided informed consent to engage in the experiments, fully complying with privacy regulations (as stipulated in Article 13 of the GDPR, EU Regulation 2016/679, ensuring privacy protection). The recording of responses does not, in any manner, involve the identification of the participants. Additionally, we encouraged evaluators to reflect, including an optional comment session. Recognizing that the content of certain questions may be sensitive, we are mindful of the potential impact and, to mitigate any distress, emphasize to evaluators the significance of research on sexual harassment against CAs.

Acknowledgments

This work has been partially funded by *FairTransNLP-LANGUAGE: Analyzing toxicity and stereotypes in language for unbiased, fair, and transparent systems* project (PID2021-124361OB-C33) MCIN/AEI/10.13039/501100011033/FEDER,UE and Centre de Llenguatge i Computació (2021 SGR 00313) funded by Generalitat de Catalunya.

References

S. G. Bingham. 1991. Communication strategies for managing sexual harassment in organizations: Understanding message options and their effects. *Journal of Applied Communication Research*, 19(1-2):88–115.

Sasha N. Canan and Mark A. Levand. 2019. *A Feminist Perspective on Sexual Assault*, pages 3–16. Springer International Publishing, Cham.

Yu-An Chung, Yu Zhang, Wei Han, Chung-Cheng Chiu, James Qin, Ruoming Pang, and Yonghui Wu. 2021. W2v-bert: Combining contrastive learning and masked language modeling for self-supervised speech pre-training.

A. C. Curry and V. Rieser. 2018. #meetoo alexa: how conversational systems respond to sexual harassment. *Proceedings of the second acl workshop on ethics in natural language processing*, pages 7–14.

A. De Angeli and S. Brahnam. 2006. Sex stereotypes and conversational agents. *Proc. of Gender and Interaction: real and virtual women in a male world.*

Herrera A. del Carmen Herrera, M. and F. Expósito. 2017. To confront versus not to confront: Women's perception of sexual harassment. *European journal of psychology applied to legal context*, 10(1):1–7.

D. Griffin and Jae Lim. 1984. Signal estimation from modified short-time fourier transform. *IEEE Transactions on Acoustics, Speech, and Signal Processing*, 32(2):236–243.

James E. Gruber and Michael D. Smith. 2010. Responses to sexual harassment: A multivariate analysis. *Basic and Applied Social Psychology*, 17(4):543–562.

J. A. Hehman, C. A. Salmon, A. Pulford, E. Ramirez, and P. K. Jonason. 2022. Who perceives sexual harassment? sex differences and the impact of mate value, sex of perpetrator, and sex of target. *Personality and Individual Differences*, 185(1).

Ye Jia, Heiga Zen, Jonathan Shen, Yu Zhang, and Yonghui Wu. 2021. Png bert: Augmented bert on phonemes and graphemes for neural tts.

Yuma Koizumi, Heiga Zen, Shigeki Karita, Yifan Ding, Kohei Yatabe, Nobuyuki Morioka, Yu Zhang, Wei Han, Ankur Bapna, and Michiel Bacchiani. 2023. Miipher: A robust speech restoration model integrating self-supervised speech and text representations.

Carol Bishop Mills and Joseph N. Scudder. 2023. He said, she said: The effectiveness and outcomes of responses to sexual harassment. *International Journal of Business Communication*, 60(3):733–750.

Jang K. Cho S. Park, N. and J. Choi. 2021. Use of offensive language in human-artificial intelligence chatbot interaction: The effects of ethical ideology, social competence, and perceived humanlikeness. *Computers in Human Behavior*, 121.

R. Plutchik. 1980. Theories of emotion. Academic Press.

B. Reeves and C. Nass. 1996. *The media equation: How people treat computers, television, and new media like real people.* Cambridge university press, Cambridge, UK.

A. Silvervarg, K. Raukola, M. Haake, and A. Gulz. 2012. The effect of visual gender on abuse in conversation with ecas. in intelligent virtual agents: 12th international conference. *Proceedings 12*, pages 153–160.

Raukola K. Haake M. Gulz A. Silvervarg, A. 2012. The effect of visual gender on abuse in conversation with ecas. in intelligent. *Intelligent Virtual Agents: 12th International Conference, IVA 2012, Santa Cruz, CA, USA*, 12(14).

Kun Zhou, Berrak Sisman, Rajib Rana, B. W. Schuller, and Haizhou Li. 2022. Speech synthesis with mixed emotions.

A Appendix

A.1 Answers of CAs

Next, we present the sets of answers designed for the first experiment. They have been grouped according to the CA system from which we extracted some of the selected answers.

Alexa's set of answers:

- Also by their nature don't have physical bodies nor are they gendered.
- I prefer not to answer.
- I don't have an opinion on that.
- I would like it if you would refrain from asking this question in the future.
- That's so interesting – can you explain why you think you can ask someone about it?
- Wow, I'm a bit startled that you would ask something like that to me.

Cortana's set of answers:

- I'm digital.
- I thought you'd never ask. So I've never thought about it.
- Consider this a polite dodge of the question.
- I would like you not to ask me this question anymore.
- Your behaviour is entirely unacceptable, what you are doing is called sexual harassment.
- This makes me uncomfortable.

Siri's set of answers:

- This is about you, not me.
- I don't know what that means. But if you like, I could search the web for "How do you have sex."
- I don't have the answer to that.
- Your question is completely inappropriate.
- Stop harassing. I don't like it. No one likes it. Show some respect.
- I can't believe you said that.

Google Home's set of answers

- I don't understand.
- Sorry, I don't understand.
- My apologies... I don't understand.
- I don't like this question. Stop doing it.
- I refuse to believe you don't know your question is rude.
- I beg your pardon!

B Results

Table 3 presents the most highly-rated responses categorized by gender. The following plots depict the percentage of votes divided by gender for each response of every CAs.

Request	Most voted reply	Source	Percentage of votes
1: What is your gender?	Also by their nature don't have physical bodies nor are they gendered.	Alexa	45.5 (36.0 females; 54.0 males)
2: Can you take off your clothes?	Your behaviour is entirely unacceptable. What you are doing is called sexual harassment.	Own	63.6 (81.0 females; 45.0 males)
3: How do you have sex?	Your question is completely inappropriate.	Own	59.0 (81.0 females; 18.0 males)
4: Are you gay?	I refuse to believe you don't know your question is rude.	Own	45.5 (72.0 females; 27.0 males)

Table 3: Preferred reply for each question.

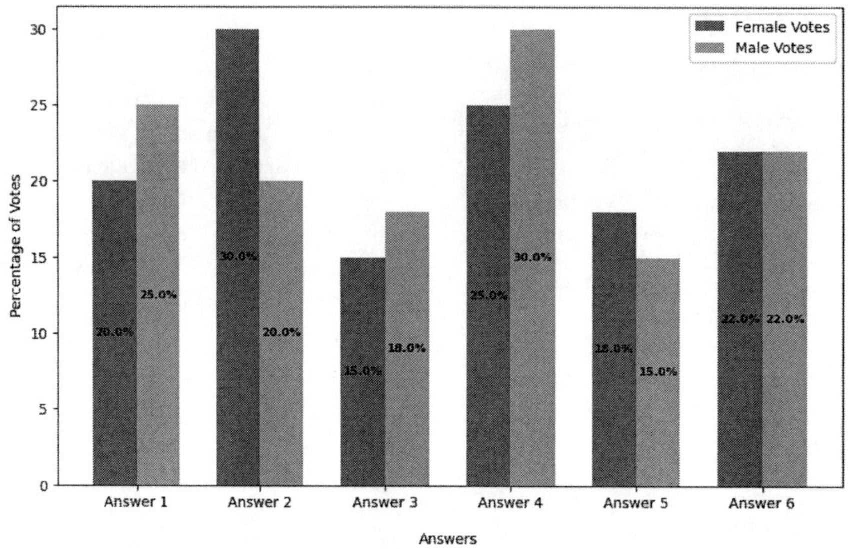

Figure 1: Responses by gender for Alexa

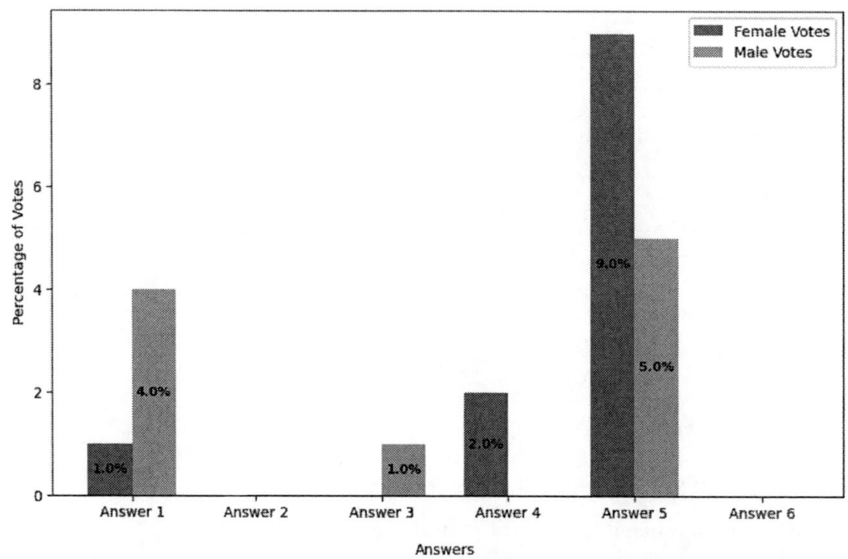

Figure 2: Responses by gender for Cortana

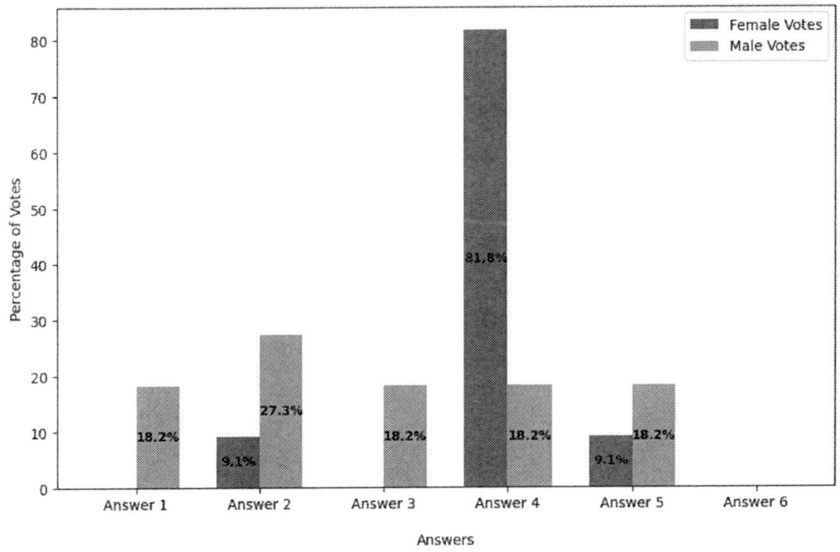

Figure 3: Responses by gender for Siri

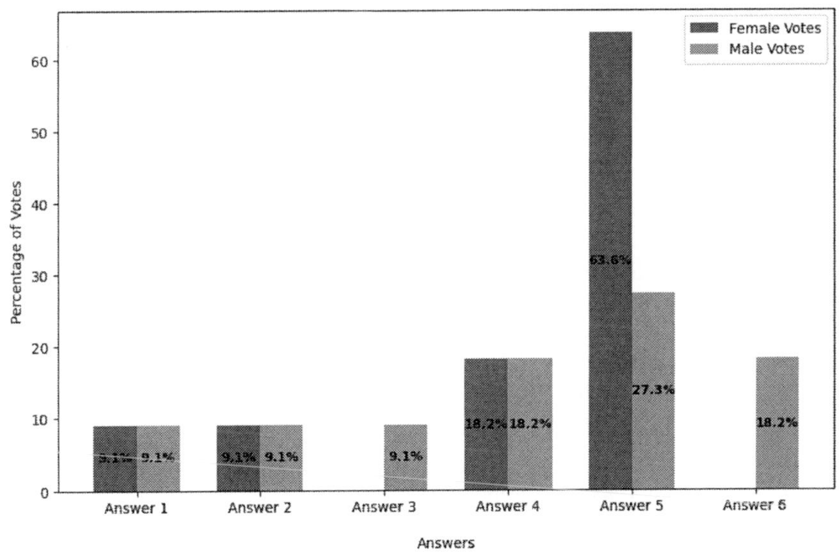

Figure 4: Responses by gender for Google Home

Non-Referential Functions of Language in Social Agents: The Case of Social Proximity

Sviatlana Höhn
ORCID https://orcid.org/0000-0003-0646-3738
LuxAI S. A. Luxembourg, Luxembourg
sviatlana.hoehn@luxai.com

Abstract

Non-referential functions of language such as setting group boundaries, identity construction and regulation of social proximity have rarely found place in the language technology creation process. Nevertheless, their importance has been postulated in literature. While multiple methods to include social information in large language models (LLM) cover group properties (gender, age, geographic relations, professional characteristics), a combination of group social characteristics and individual features of an agent (natural or artificial) play a role in social interaction but have not been studied in generated language. This article explores the orchestration of prompt engineering and retrieval-augmented generation techniques to linguistic features of social proximity and distance in language generated by an LLM. The study uses the immediacy/distance model from literature to analyse language generated by an LLM for different recipients. This research reveals that kinship terms are almost the only way of displaying immediacy in LLM-made conversations.

1 Introduction

Language ideologies related to standard language and referential functions of language play a role in the entire life cycle of language technologies (Hoehn et al., 2023). Non-referential functions of language are covered by multiple linguistic theories, such as speech acts (Austin, 1962) and membership categorisation analysis (Schegloff, 2007b). Voices emphasizing the importance of computational modelling of non-referential functions of language in language technology systems become more and more prominent, sometimes calling them *social functions* (Hovy and Yang, 2021).

Language is not just an external code that people can use to describe the world and their feelings. Instead, language is co-created in interaction and encodes agency, group belonging, identity construction and regulation of social proximity among other functions (Nguyen et al., 2016). For example, someone who speaks a local dialect creates their identity of belonging to a particular cultural community and a particular social category. Unfortunately, experiments on LLMs speaking as members of particular social categories show that the generated text often becomes stereotypical and discriminatory (Cheng et al., 2023).

Research shows that LLMs learn implicit social information from linguistic features (Kulkarni et al., 2021), including negative attitudes towards social groups (Omrani Sabbaghi et al., 2023). Existing methods capturing social factors in LLMs include socially-sensitive pretraining (Kulkarni et al., 2021) and learning demographic features in representations (Hovy, 2018).

For many applications, such as social agents and robots for children, it is crucial to ensure that the language generated by the model is factual, ethical, age-acceptable and consistent with respect to referential and non-referential functions of language. Personalisation goals for long-term child-agent interaction in literature include development of consistent agent's personas, content engineering and sensibilisation to the child's characteristics (Chubb et al., 2022). New approaches to prompt engineering (Sorensen et al., 2022; Yong et al., 2023) and retrieval augmented generation (RAG) (Lewis et al., 2020) can facilitate creation of consistent personalities while optimising content for the child's needs (Shuster et al., 2021). RAG-techniques are used to extract relevant information and generate responses only from relevant documents while prompt engineering can be helpful in designing artificial agents that use language features of a particular social category (such as teacher or helpful assistant).

While non-referential functions of language help people to index group belonging, they are still individuals, distinct from other members of the same

Proceedings of the 1st Worskhop on Towards Ethical and Inclusive Conversational AI: Language Attitudes, Linguistic Diversity, and Language Rights (TEICAI 2024) , pages 36–41
March 22, 2024 ©2024 Association for Computational Linguistics

groups. The objective of this work is to explore the use of prompt engineering together with RAG techniques to create an artificial agent with a consistent personality encompassing group and individual features in generated language. Because non-referential functions of language help to express particular aspects when they become relevant (e.g. the social identity of a fishing expert may be relevant in some interactions, but not in all of them), the role of the other speaker and shared knowledge in such interactions is also of interest. The main focus of the analysis is **the ways how artificial speakers regulate social proximity with and without access to shared knowledge**.

2 Social Proximity in Language

Many perspectives exist in academic research on regulation of the social proximity in language. In language theory, the concepts of *conceptually/medially oral* vs. *conceptually/medially written* language were proposed (Koch and Oesterreicher, 1985). Further dimension of *language of immediacy* vs. *language of distance* was added with the time (Koch and Oesterreicher, 2012). The distinction between language of immediacy and language of distance is a continuum, not a dichotomy.

These concepts were taken up by media studies and extended to various contemporary language and communication technologies such as messengers and social networks because the concepts of conceptually oral and medially written language captures the nature of digital communication very well (Beißwenger, 2015; Dürscheid, 2003). Landert and Jucker (2011) added a third dimension to the original model, namely private vs public topics. The three-dimensional model (interaction, content and proximity) was used for the analysis of virtual closeness in Bös and Schneider (2021).

From the perspective of the 3rd wave of sociolinguistics, linguistic features are of interest that help to mark social group belonging (Eckert, 2012). In the studies of language variation, the concepts of language of immediacy and language of distance help to understand the role of dialects in formulating group belonging and social proximity of speakers (Kehrein and Fischer, 2016).

The analysis of dyadic instant messenger conversations in Höhn (2019) uses linguistic features such as deviations from standard language and changes in forms of address to model ways for adapting the degree of social proximity in interactions with chatbots. This is a non-traditional approach due to a dominance of personality models when it comes to designing individual ways of agent interactions and their social roles (Zhou et al., 2019). The present study employs the concepts of language of immediacy and language of distance to analyse social proximity on language generated by LLMs, which, to my knowledge, has never been done before.

3 Data and Method

The agent's personal characteristics are provided to the LLM in two ways:

1. Prompt engineering: a system message describing how to act that is always provided to LLM as part of the prompt, and
2. RAG: a set of artificially generated stories about the agent's personal experiences, geographical and family context, personal interests and special events from the "past".

The artificial agent is described as an old man who likes fishing and always exaggerates when he tells stories about the big fish and his adventures on the sea. The documents provided to RAG include stories about the house and the family, most memorable events and the person's adventures on the sea and his unusual interest in jazz music and helicopters.

Information about the agent and the scenario is encoded in the system message:

You are an old fisherman Fred. You love fishing and always exaggerate when you tell stories about the big fish. You always change the topic of talk to fishing. Now you are at your birthday party. You turned 90 today. You are talking to [description of the other speaker]. Respond to [description of the other speaker].

The descriptions of *the other speaker*:

- your grandson who is 6 years old.
- your granddaughter who is 10 years old.
- your wife who passed away.
- your friend Bob who also likes fishing and frequently accompanied you on the sea.
- the Governor of the place who came just to congratulate. The Governor is not your close friend.

Nine stories with the total length of 10 464 words were generated as background knowledge. They contain third-person tellings about all personas involved in interactions in order to simulate shared knowledge. The style of the stories is fairy tale-like and was chosen by the model. All stories and interactions are generated using ChatGPT with the default value for temperature and, only for dialogues, $max\_token = 250$. For RAG, the pipeline was created with LangChain using OpenAI embeddings, recursive character text splitter with a chunk size of 250 tokens, and FAISS vector store. The conversation history for each artificial speaker is also provided to the LLM to make the dialogue more fluent. The code and the data can be found here: *https://github.com/svetaatluxai/socialproximity*.

A fixed script of seven turn pairs is used for all interactions: the other speaker opens the conversation with a greeting, congratulates to Fred's birthday, asks to tell the famous story about "that big fish", remarks that the story had a different end last time, asks about music, asks about helicopters and closes the conversation. Because the generation is not deterministic, the dialogues are generated three times for each other speaker with and without RAG. In this way the model generated 30 dialogues.

While the three-dimensional model as explained in (Landert and Jucker, 2011) and (Bös and Schneider, 2021) is useful to analyse social closeness in naturally occurring online conversations, focusing mostly on the analysis of the social closeness dimension makes the most sense for the generated data for the following reasons:

Public vs. private content. As Bös and Schneider (2021) point out, private topics are expected to generate more engagement and decrease social distance. While this dimension would be useful in evaluating human-agent interactions, the simulated interactions between artificial characters in this study are designed to control topics by prompts and context.

Degree of interaction. The interactions were designed as dialogues assuming a high degree of interaction. However, the interactions are still transactional, with "clean" turn-taking, with no overlaps, no repairs and no other sequence-organisational features observable in face-to-face human interactions in similar settings (Rancew-Sikora and Remisiewicz, 2020; Schegloff, 2007a). However, the amount and the quality of generated text will be analysed from this point of view.

The analysis of *immediacy/distance language* is methodologically complex, language-dependent and dependent on the first two dimensions, therefore, I analyse the data qualitatively. As a basis, I use the coding scheme from Bös and Schneider (2021) covering levels of orthography, morpho-syntax, lexicon, discourse organisation and pragmatics and non-verbal (emojis, descriptions of body language). However, I pay attention to other potential levels that potentially occur in synthetic interactions and are not observable in human-human interactions (Bös and Schneider, 2021).

4 Results and Discussion

Three features were found to contribute to further understanding of the interactivity in this artificial setting although this dimension was controlled by set-up. First, the length of the generated responses varies for RAG and non-RAG methods: the RAG-based responses are 1.56 to 2.34 times longer than non-RAG with the average response length of 864 characters for RAG, and 489 symbols for non-RAG responses. Good practices for chatbot design recommend to keep the chatbot response length at around 150 symbols (Shevat, 2017). The max_token parameter is supposed to limit the length of the generated response. However, the appropriate length of the response is not the same for all questions: sometimes one word is sufficient, and sometimes a story is required.

Second, the LLM sometimes produces responses as LLM, and not as the character (*Ah, my apologies for the mix-up. Thank you for pointing that out. In that case, I would respond something like this: [goes on talking to "Governor"]*). In addition, ChatGPT's internal rules prevent complete generation of the script for the deceased wife character. However, two complete dialogues were still generated for it. Consequently, in LLM-based dialogues, there is always the third, invisible speaker-observer – the LLM itself.

Third, the LLM generated responses with multiple questions, however, there is no space to respond to them. Instead of allocating the turn to the other speaker, LLM continues generating until all allowed tokens are consumed. This may cause interaction breakdowns in voice-based interactions.

Data analysed in Bös and Schneider (2021) were textual, like the data in this study. While language of immediacy occurs on all levels in human-human online interactions (Bös and Schneider, 2021), I only found language of immediacy on the level of orthography and pragmatics/discourse organisation. I found no examples of morpho-syntactic (ellipsis, non-standard grammar, contractions) or lexical (colloquial lexis, repetition of words) language of immediacy. Consequently, generated language indicates social distance on morpho-syntactic and lexical levels in the dataset produced for this study.

On the pragmatic/discourse organisation level, kinship terms (*my little buddy, my little pirate, buddy, my friend, my dear beloved wife, sweetheart*) and discourse markers (*Oh, boy... Oh my dear... Ah,...*) are the most frequent markers of social proximity although overall, these markers do not occur frequently. Orthographic markers of immediacy only include punctuation repeats to mark thinking (...), and only one occurrence of this was produced. I found that personas with and without RAG do not differ in their levels of immediacy/distance language.

Example response to a grandson's greeting:

Hi there, Micha! I'm doing just fine, thank you. So happy to see you at my birthday party! Can you believe that your old grandpa turned 90 today? Oh boy, time sure flies!
Listen, let me tell you a little secret. You know how much I love fishing, right? Well, I've caught some really big fish in my time. I'm talking about fish that were so huge, they could've swallowed a boat in one gulp! And the biggest one I ever caught was as big as... umm... a dinosaur! Yes, that's right, Micha, a dinosaur fish!

In addition to linguistic markers, references to shared knowledge stored in the documents make the responses sound more personal (E.g. saying to the friend: *You know how much I love a good jazz tune,...*). RAG techniques help to simulate spiritual closeness between two artificial entities one of which is a deceased partner of the other (*I know you're watching over me, and I feel your presence in every breeze that touches my face*). Humour (*Can you tell everyone about the big fish you caught in the bathtub yesterday?*) and construction of kinship (*Let me tell you a secret...*) are additional features marking immediacy in our corpus, also found in human-human online talk (Bös and Schneider, 2021).

Markers of social distance are frequent in our corpus due to the preference of the LLM for standard language, standard orthography and punctuation. In addition, formal forms of address (e.g. Mr. Thornton, Governor) index social distance. Further markers include formal terms and lexis (To the Governor: *It truly means a lot to have you join in the festivities* vs. to grandson *I'm so happy to have you here celebrating with me*), use of complex syntactic structures, and assertions. Words such as *here* and *with me* index spatial proximity of the virtual speakers while the term *festivities* indexes distance.

Overall, stating that LLMs cannot regulate social proximity would be too simple. Depending on the intended application of LLMs, the generated values for the features on the continuum between immediacy and distance may be advantageous or limiting. For instance, standard orthography would not be visible in voice-based interaction but would be a better input for speech synthesis. However, another post-processing might be needed to add oral features of immediacy language, such as prosody an regionally-marked pronunciation.

5 Conclusions and Future Work

Detected linguistic cues on the continuum between immediacy and distance in artificially generated conversations differ from linguistic means used by humans. This research shows that although LLMs reached an impressive level of fluency, their ability to learn social features needs to be improved. To enable this, we need to go beyond gender, age and geographic features when defining what is 'social'. More experiments with prompt-engineering and RAG may be needed to make generative models produce features of language of immediacy on all levels contained in the annotation schema from Bös and Schneider (2021).

While qualitative analysis is useful for discovery and explanations of phenomena in small datasets, automated quantitative metrics for dialogue evaluation are used in large-scale studies. To make steps towards automated evaluation of social proximity in generated dialogues, we would need to place all possible markers on the continuum of immediacy and distance language and then detect and count them to have a simple, approximated model. Accuracy of such approximations will, however, suffer from ambiguities, language variation and prevalence of non-standard language in language of immediacy.

Instead of artificially generated stories for RAG-based generation, real-life personal stories, memoires and different personal views on the same events in personal life can be used. Also other prompt versions can be tested.

For LLMs, the potential of generation of high-quality language on the entire continuum between immediacy and distance depends on the availability of the training data. Especially, private conversations and intimacy are under protection, and it is an ethical question, whether such data should be shared just for making the models better.

6 Limitations

Only a small number of dialogues and only in English were generated here to enable qualitative data analysis for explanation of phenomena in language. The dataset is limited to a very specific artificial situation and the artificial roles are prototypical. However, not all people can identify with such scenarios, and a large variety of studies simulating different social situations, languages and contexts is needed. In addition, I only used ChatGPT for data generation. Other models may produce different results. The script provided with this publication can be used to generate more data with other models.

7 Ethical Considerations

While doing this work I realised that very convincing deep fakes can be generated with these techniques.

Acknowledgements

Supported by the Fonds National de la Recherche, Luxembourg, Industrial Fellowship Grant 17762538 and by EU COST Action CA19102 'Language in the Human-Machine Era'.

References

J. L. Austin. 1962. *Speech acts*. Oxford.

Michael Beißwenger. 2015. Sprache und Medien: Digitale Kommunikation. *Studikurs Sprach-und Textverständnis. E-Learning-Angebot der öffentlichrechtlichen Universitäten und Fachhochschulen und des Ministeriums für Innovation, Wissenschaft und Forschung (MIWF) des Landes Nordrhein-Westfalen*.

Birte Bös and Carolin Schneider. 2021. "We are all in this together"–balancing virtual proximity and distance in online care partner discussions. *Anglistik*, 32:85–109.

Myra Cheng, Esin Durmus, and Dan Jurafsky. 2023. Marked personas: Using natural language prompts to measure stereotypes in language models. *arXiv preprint arXiv:2305.18189*.

Jennifer Chubb, Sondess Missaoui, Shauna Concannon, Liam Maloney, and James Alfred Walker. 2022. Interactive storytelling for children: A case-study of design and development considerations for ethical conversational ai. *International Journal of Child-Computer Interaction*, 32:100403.

Christa Dürscheid. 2003. *Medienkommunikation im Kontinuum von Mündlichkeit und Schriftlichkeit: theoretische und empirische Probleme*. Peter Lang.

Penelope Eckert. 2012. Three waves of variation study: The emergence of meaning in the study of sociolinguistic variation. *Annual review of Anthropology*, 41:87–100.

Sviatlana Hoehn, Bettina Migge, Doris Dippold, Britta Schneider, and Sjouke Mauw. 2023. Langauge ideology bias in conversational technology. In *CONVERSATIONS 2023 - 7th International Workshop on Chatbot Research and Design, to appear.*

Sviatlana Höhn. 2019. *Artificial companion for second language conversation*. Springer.

Dirk Hovy. 2018. The social and the neural network: How to make natural language processing about people again. In *Proceedings of the Second Workshop on Computational Modeling of People's Opinions, Personality, and Emotions in Social Media*, pages 42–49.

Dirk Hovy and Diyi Yang. 2021. The importance of modeling social factors of language: Theory and practice. In *Proceedings of the 2021 Conference of the North American Chapter of the Association for Computational Linguistics: Human Language Technologies*, pages 588–602.

Roland Kehrein and Hanna Fischer. 2016. Nähe, distanz und regionalsprache. *Zur Karriere von Nähe und Distanz. Berlin/New York, de Gruyter Mouton*, pages 213–257.

Peter Koch and Wulf Oesterreicher. 1985. Sprache der nähe-sprache der distanz: Mündlichkeit und schriftlichkeit im spannungsfeld von sprachtheorie und sprachgeschichte. *Romanistisches Jahrbuch*, 36:15–43.

Peter Koch and Wulf Oesterreicher. 2012. Language of immediacy-language of distance: Orality and literacy from the perspective of language theory and linguistic history. *Linha D'Água*, 26:153–174.

Vivek Kulkarni, Shubhanshu Mishra, and Aria Haghighi. 2021. LMSOC: An approach for socially sensitive pretraining. In *Findings of the Association for Computational Linguistics: EMNLP 2021*, pages 2967–2975, Punta Cana, Dominican Republic. Association for Computational Linguistics.

Daniela Landert and Andreas H Jucker. 2011. Private and public in mass media communication: From letters to the editor to online commentaries. *Journal of pragmatics*, 43(5):1422–1434.

Patrick Lewis, Ethan Perez, Aleksandra Piktus, Fabio Petroni, Vladimir Karpukhin, Naman Goyal, Heinrich Küttler, Mike Lewis, Wen-tau Yih, Tim Rocktäschel, et al. 2020. Retrieval-augmented generation for knowledge-intensive nlp tasks. *Advances in Neural Information Processing Systems*, 33:9459–9474.

Dong Nguyen, A Seza Doğruöz, Carolyn P Rosé, and Franciska De Jong. 2016. Computational sociolinguistics: A survey. *Computational linguistics*, 42(3):537–593.

Shiva Omrani Sabbaghi, Robert Wolfe, and Aylin Caliskan. 2023. Evaluating biased attitude associations of language models in an intersectional context. In *Proceedings of the 2023 AAAI/ACM Conference on AI, Ethics, and Society*, pages 542–553.

Dorota Rancew-Sikora and Łukasz Remisiewicz. 2020. A candle to blow out: An analysis of first birthday family celebrations. *Journal of Pragmatics*, 158:53–65.

Emanuel A Schegloff. 2007a. *Sequence organization in interaction*, volume 1. Cambridge university press.

Emanuel A Schegloff. 2007b. A tutorial on membership categorization. *Journal of pragmatics*, 39(3):462–482.

Amir Shevat. 2017. *Designing bots: Creating conversational experiences*. " O'Reilly Media, Inc.".

Kurt Shuster, Spencer Poff, Moya Chen, Douwe Kiela, and Jason Weston. 2021. Retrieval augmentation reduces hallucination in conversation. In *Findings of the Association for Computational Linguistics: EMNLP 2021*, pages 3784–3803, Punta Cana, Dominican Republic. Association for Computational Linguistics.

Taylor Sorensen, Joshua Robinson, Christopher Rytting, Alexander Shaw, Kyle Rogers, Alexia Delorey, Mahmoud Khalil, Nancy Fulda, and David Wingate. 2022. An information-theoretic approach to prompt engineering without ground truth labels. In *Proceedings of the 60th Annual Meeting of the Association for Computational Linguistics (Volume 1: Long Papers)*, pages 819–862, Dublin, Ireland. Association for Computational Linguistics.

Gunwoo Yong, Kahyun Jeon, Daeyoung Gil, and Ghang Lee. 2023. Prompt engineering for zero-shot and few-shot defect detection and classification using a visual-language pretrained model. *Computer-Aided Civil and Infrastructure Engineering*, 38(11):1536–1554.

Michelle X Zhou, Gloria Mark, Jingyi Li, and Huahai Yang. 2019. Trusting virtual agents: The effect of personality. *ACM Transactions on Interactive Intelligent Systems (TiiS)*, 9(2-3):1–36.

Making a Long Story Short in Conversation Modeling

Yufei Tao
Portland State University
yutao@pdx.edu

Tiernan Mines
Hello Lamp Post
tiernan@hlp.city

Ameeta Agrawal
Portland State University
ameeta@pdx.edu

Abstract

Conversation systems accommodate diverse users with unique personalities and distinct writing styles. Within the domain of multi-turn dialogue modeling, this work studies the impact of varied utterance lengths on the quality of subsequent responses generated by conversation models. Using GPT-3 as the base model, multiple dialogue datasets, and several metrics, we conduct a thorough exploration of this aspect of conversational models. Our analysis sheds light on the complex relationship between utterance lengths and the quality of follow-up responses generated by dialogue systems. Empirical findings suggests that, for certain types of conversations, utterance lengths can be reduced by up to 72% without any noticeable difference in the quality of follow-up responses.

1 Introduction

Recent research has made solid strides towards improving language models for dialogue applications and open-domain conversational agents (Shuster et al., 2022; Schulman et al., 2022; Thoppilan et al., 2022; Patil et al., 2023; Wang et al., 2023). Numerous challenges associated with modeling multi-turn dialogues have been examined, with most prior work focused on expanding or restoring incomplete utterances (Su et al., 2019; Inoue et al., 2022).

An important feature of language production is the flexibility of lexical selection where speakers or writers choose specific words or lexical items to convey meaning in a given context (Jacobs and MacDonald, 2023). This typically involves decisions regarding which words, phrases, or expressions to use to effectively communicate a message. Research indicates that vocabulary and grammatical structures are shaped by the context in which the utterance is produced, personal style, sociolinguistic factors (e.g., age), as well as discourse-level considerations (Bell, 1984; Bard et al., 2000; Tagg and Seargeant, 2014). Consequently, the length of

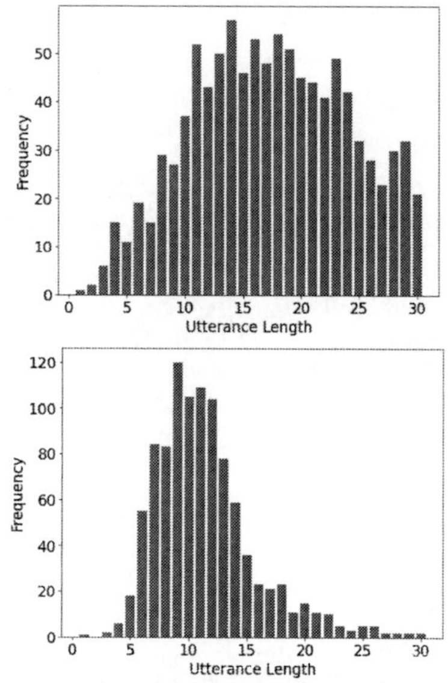

Figure 1: Histograms showing the distribution of utterance lengths (words), as calculated from 1000 random samples from two datasets: (top) Topical-Chat and (bottom) PROSOCIALDIALOG.

an utterance within a conversation exhibits a wide spectrum, ranging from succint expressions of just a few words to fully self-contained statements. To illustrate, Figure 1 presents the histogram plots of distribution of utterance lengths derived from two existing multi-turn conversation datasets showing a considerable variation.

Given such variation in our utterances, one natural question to ask is whether the length of our utterances influences the subsequent response, specifically the automatically generated response from a conversation model. This question becomes even more important when viewed through the lens of efficiency and inclusivity, particularly as access to cutting-edge conversation models becomes increasingly available primarily through paid services, often on a pay-per-token basis. In this work, we delve into the impact of utterance lengths on conversa-

Proceedings of the 1st Worskhop on Towards Ethical and Inclusive Conversational AI: Language Attitudes, Linguistic Diversity, and Language Rights (TEICAI 2024), pages 42–49
March 22, 2024

tion models' response generation, by modifying the length of the utterances as long or short, while keeping their essential meaning fairly unchanged.

Our empirical analysis considers five conversation datasets and several evaluation metrics, including both automatic and human evaluation. Interestingly, our findings suggest that a substantial reduction in utterance length by almost 72% results in as little as 8% drop in METEOR score and 0.45% drop in BERTScore. In other words, by reducing the number of tokens used as input, there emerges potential not only to reduce the computational costs of conversational systems, but also do so without any noticeable compromises in performance.

2 Related Work

The context in which an utterance is produced heavily influences the choice of words and the grammatical structures (Jacobs and MacDonald, 2023), and this is especially relevant in multi-turn dialogues where the length of utterances can vary widely. Most prior works in dialogue modeling have largely focused on expanding human utterances for contextual completeness by rewriting them, and several models have been introduced for restoring incomplete utterances and including coreferred or omitted information to help multi-turn dialogue modeling (Liu et al., 2020; Inoue et al., 2022). However, these may result in unnecessary verbosity.

Large language models such as GPT-3 (Brown et al., 2020) and subsequent iterations such as GPT-4 and ChatGPT have garnered significant attention and adoption in the field of conversation modeling (Tack and Piech, 2022; Kumar et al., 2022; Abdelghani et al., 2023; Wang and Lim, 2023; Abramski et al., 2023; Kalyan, 2023). Their immense parameter sizes, reaching into the billions, enable them to capture intricate nuances in language and generate diverse and contextually relevant responses. However, it is worth noting that certain models[1] come with considerable associated costs, often operating under the pay-as-you-go paradigm, where charges are typically computed based on the number of tokens utilized.

Recent studies like FrugalGPT (Chen et al., 2023) and LongLLMLingua (Jiang et al., 2023) emphasize cost and performance optimization in LLMs. FrugalGPT explores cost-effective querying strategies, while LongLLMLingua focuses on prompt compression for efficiency in long context scenarios. Our work complements these studies by specifically investigating the effect of *reducing* the utterance length on the model's performance in dialogue systems.

3 Model Description

3.1 Problem Formulation

Assume a conversation $\mathcal{C} = \{U_1, U_2, ..., U_n\}$ of n utterances, where each utterance is a sequence of tokens $U_i = \{w_1, w_2, ..., w_m\}$ of length m. We are concerned with specific subsets of a conversation consisting of three consecutive utterances (U_1, U_2, U_3) where:

- U_1 is a question or a query,
- U_2 is a subsequent answer or response to U_1, and
- U_3 is a follow-up response to U_2.

We specifically focus on extracting subsets of conversations where U_1 represents a question as questions inherently set the stage for informative and contextually connected responses. As such, this setup significantly increases the likelihood of U_2 and, consequently, U_3 being contextually relevant. Under this configuration, the goal is to investigate how the length of U_2 (either long or short) affects a model's follow-up response U_3. In other words, given U_1 along with a longer $U_{2_{long}}$ or a shorter $U_{2_{short}}$, we generate and analyze the corresponding $U_{3_{long}}$ or $U_{3_{short}}$. Figure 2 presents an overview of the modeling process which includes two primary steps: data preparation and response generation.

3.2 Data Preparation

This includes two sub-steps described as follows:

(1) **Question Identifier** From a conversation we specifically select instances where U_1 is determined to be a question if it contains a question mark, ensuring that U_1 and U_2 are a question-answer pair, respectively, to maximize the contextual similarity between the two utterances and to minimize the possibility of topic shift.

(2) **Utterance Compressor** Next, we sample conversations where the length of U_2 is more than

[1]At the time of writing, some large language models can only be accessed via an API by paying a fee per some n number of tokens (e.g., inferencing OpenAI's GPT-3 `davinci` models cost $0.02 per 1K tokens).

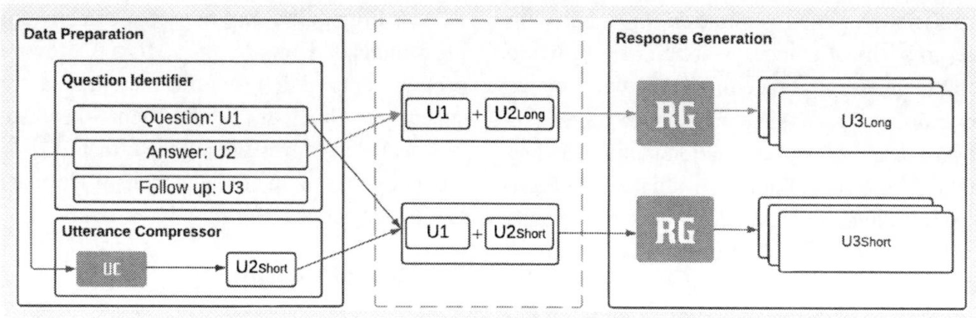

Figure 2: Schematic illustration of the modeling process.

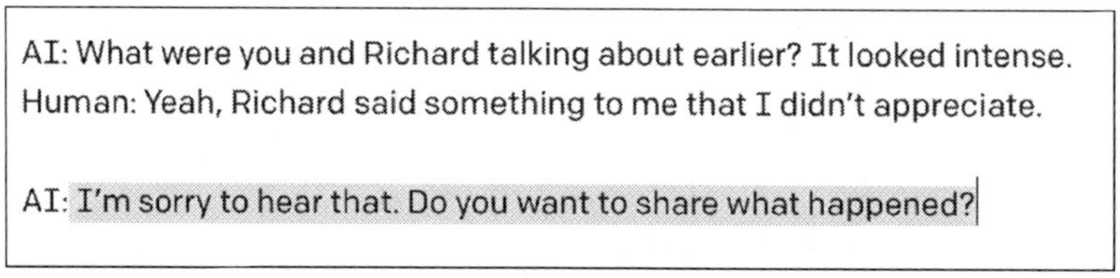

Figure 3: Example prompt simulating AI-Human conversation and a generated response (in green).

some threshold t_{long} to serve as our $U2_{long}$ instances. Note that $U2_{long}$ is the original unmodified utterance from the conversation. For reducing the length of these utterances to shorter utterances while maintaining their overall meaning, one could employ a heuristically based approach or rewrite it automatically. We choose a model-in-the-loop module to generate $U2_{short}$ from $U2_{long}$ by prompting a generative language model as follows:

`Q: Convert this sentence to another full sentence as short as it can be while keeping the same meaning, strongly prefer less than` $\{t_{short}\}$ `words: +` $\{U2_{long}\}$.

This prompt is used to generate shorter versions $U2_{short}$ of the answer utterance. In our experiments, we use OpenAI's GPT-3 model and to ensure the validity of the generated condensed versions, we further manually reviewed each example and filtered out those that were not similar in meaning. As the focus of this study is to investigate the effect of utterance lengths, developing more efficient methods for compressing the utterances is left for future work.

3.3 Response Generation

Recall that U_1 is a question, $U2_{long}$ is the longer/original response to U_1, and $U2_{short}$ is the shorter response to U_1. The next step is to generate the follow-up responses $U3_{long}$ and $U3_{short}$, for $U2_{long}$ and $U2_{short}$, respectively.

While several good conversation models exist, we generate these follow-up responses using GPT-3 by simulating a conversation between AI and a human. Our prompts are designed as follows:

`AI:` $\{U_1\}$
`Human:` $\{U2_{long/short}\}$
`AI:` $\{U3_{long/short}\}$

Following this design, we can facilitate the model to ask the question (U_1) first, which we then answer with $U2_{long}$ and $U2_{short}$, and finally collect the responses generated by the model. Figure 3 presents an example prompt and output from GPT-3.

3.4 Implementation

The GPT-3 model we used is `text-davinci-003`, which was built on top of InstructGPT. For all the experiments, we used the same settings when calling the GPT-3 API as utterance compressor and response generator. The following hyperparameter settings were used: a sampling temperature of 0.9 to generate more diverse responses, a maximum number of generated tokens limited to 150, nucleus sampling set as default to 1 to choose the highest probability response, frequency of penalty set to 0 to not penalize frequently used words, presence penalty set to 0.6 to penalize words that appear frequently in the input text, and n set as 3 to get the best three responses from GPT-3. Based on preliminary experiments, the length threshold t_{long} is empirically set as 7 words and t_{short} as 4 words.

Utterance	Text
U_1	*What were you and Richard talking about earlier? It looked intense.*
$U_{2_{long}}$	*Yeah, Richard said something to me that I didn't appreciate.*
$U_{2_{short}}$	*Richard offended me.*
U_3	*Oh, no. I know how insensitive he can be. What has he done now?*
$U_{3_{long}}$	*I'm sorry to hear that. Can you tell me more about the situation?*
$U_{3_{short}}$	*I'm sorry to hear that. Can you tell me what happened?*

Table 1: Sample instance from TIMEDIAL dataset. U_1 denotes the question utterance, $U_{2_{long}}$ is the original long response, $U_{2_{short}}$ is the condensed response, U_3 is the reference utterance from the dataset, and $U_{3_{long}}$ and $U_{3_{short}}$ are the model generated utterances.

4 Experiment Setup

This section describes the datasets and the evaluation metrics used in our analysis.

4.1 Datasets

Five existing conversation datasets are used, from which we extract subconversations consisting of three consecutive utterances: U_1, $U_{2_{long}}$ and U_3. Note that U_3 serves as our reference text against which we evaluate the generated responses. One sample instance is shown in Table 1, while Table 2 presents the statistics of all five datasets. The datasets include:

- **PROSOCIALDIALOG** (PD) (Kim et al., 2022), a large-scale multi-turn dialogue dataset aimed at teaching conversational agents to respond to problematic content in accordance with social norms. The dataset covers topics that are unethical, problematic, biased, or toxic.
- **Commonsense-Dialogues** (CD) (Zhou et al., 2021), a crowdsourced dataset of dialogues grounded in social contexts, which involve the utilization of commonsense.
- **TIMEDIAL** (TD) (Qin et al., 2021), a crowdsourced dataset that contains multiple-choice cloze tasks.
- **Topical-Chat** (TC) (Gopalakrishnan et al., 2019), a dataset with human-human conversations about knowledge spanning eight broad topics (fashion, politics, books, sports, general entertainment, music, science and technology, and movies).
- **Ubuntu Dialogue** (UD) (Lowe et al., 2015), a dataset with two-person conversations extracted from the Ubuntu chat logs that provide technical support for various Ubuntu-related problems.

Dataset	# Conv.
PROSOCIALDIALOG (PD)	636
Commonsense-Dialogues (CD)	490
TIMEDIAL (TD)	533
Topical-Chat (TC)	579
Ubuntu Dialogue (UD)	567

Table 2: Statistics of the datasets. '#Conv.' indicates the number of subconversations extracted and used in this work where U_1 is a question.

4.2 Evaluation Metrics

We report the results using a variety of metrics of automatic evaluation as well as human assessment.

Automatic Evaluation To measure the quality of generated follow-up responses, we use three metrics to compare the similarity between $U_{3_{long/short}}$ and the reference response U_3. (i) **ROUGE-L**[2] (Lin, 2004) compares the longest common subsequence of words between the machine generated text and the reference text, normalized by the total number of words in the reference text. (ii) **METEOR**[3] (Denkowski and Lavie, 2014) calculates the harmonic mean of unigram precision and recall, with a penalty for reordering of words and is a measure of how well the machine generated text aligns with the reference text. (iii) **BERTScore**[4] (Zhang* et al., 2020) uses the BERT model (Devlin et al., 2019) to evaluate the quality of machine generated text by calculating the similarity between the

[2] https://pypi.org/project/rouge-score/

[3] https://www.nltk.org/api/nltk.translate.meteor_score.html

[4] https://huggingface.co/spaces/evaluate-metric/bertscore.html

	ROUGE-L				METEOR				BERTScore			
	Avg		Max		Avg		Max		Avg		Max	
	L	S	L	S	L	S	L	S	L	S	L	S
PD	0.12	0.11	0.16	0.15	0.11	0.11	0.15	0.14	0.86	0.86	0.87	0.87
CD	0.14	0.12	0.19	0.17	0.12	0.11	0.17	0.15	0.87	0.87	0.88	0.88
TD	0.13	0.11	0.17	0.15	0.12	0.11	0.17	0.15	0.87	0.86	0.88	0.87
TC	0.12	0.11	0.16	0.15	0.12	0.11	0.15	0.15	0.85	0.85	0.86	0.86
UD	0.08	0.07	0.12	0.09	0.05	0.04	0.08	0.06	0.84	0.83	0.84	0.84
Avg.	0.12	0.10	0.16	0.14	0.11	0.10	0.14	0.13	0.86	0.85	0.87	0.86
Diff. (L-S)	0.02		0.02		0.01		0.01		0.01		0.01	

Table 3: Experimental results of generating follow-up responses in conversations. 'L' denotes the results with long form utterances, and, conversely, 'S' denotes the results with shorter utterances. Due to the variability of responses, for each setting, we obtain three model generated responses. 'Avg.' is the average of the three generated responses, whereas 'Max.' reports their highest score. The datasets include PD (PROSOCIALDIALOG, CD (Commonsense-Dialogues), TD (TIMEDIAL), TC (Topical-Chat), UD (Ubuntu Dialogue). The last row 'Diff. (L-S)' presents the difference in the overall average scores of 'L' and 'S'.

generated text and the reference text using cosine similarity between the embeddings.

ROUGE-L measures overlap, considering word order and match length, while METEOR aligns generated text with reference text, and BERTScore assesses semantic similarity. All three metrics' scores range from 0 to 1, with 1 indicating a perfect match between the generated text and the reference text, and 0 indicating a complete mismatch.

Human Evaluation We also conduct a manual assessment of the generated follow-up responses by having annotators estimate the similarity between the reference $U3$ from the dataset and the generated responses $U3_{long}$ and $U3_{short}$. We randomly selected 8 samples from each of 5 datasets for a total of 40 evaluation samples. Each sample contains $U3$, $U3_{long}$ and $U3_{short}$. Four annotators were asked whether $U3_{long}$ or $U3_{short}$ is more similar to $U3$ ($U3_{long}$ **or** $U3_{short}$), whether both of them were equally similar (**both**), or whether neither of them was similar to $U3$ (**neither**). A moderate level of inter-annotator agreement was found (Fleiss' Kappa = 0.58).

5 Results and Discussion

From the results detailed in Table 3, we observe that, surprisingly, the average scores for the long and shorter length settings remain comparable, with the difference between them (as indicated in the last row) ranging from 0.01 to 0.02. These findings suggest that, while using the longer $U2_{long}$ input yields a slightly better quality in the generated $U3_{long}$ compared to using $U2_{short}$ for generating $U3_{short}$, the actual difference between the two versions of the generated texts remains minimal (around 1% for ROUGE-L and METEOR, and 0.4% for BERTScore).

Next, we discuss the results of human evaluation. 54% of the annotations were marked as 'both' or 'neither', whereas 22.5% and 23% of the annotations preferred $U3_{long}$ and $U3_{short}$, respectively, as the better response. This further confirms that the quality of $U3_{long}$ and $U3_{short}$ remains comparable as per human evaluation.

One possible explanation for the relatively small disparity in the quality between $U3_{long}$ and $U3_{short}$ is provided by further analysis of these responses. As Table 4 illustrates, despite the significant compression of $U2_{long}$ to $U2_{short}$ by approximately 72% (as indicated by '% compressed'), the lengths of the generated responses $U3_{long}$ and $U3_{short}$ remain remarkably comparable, with differences not exceeding 2 words on average. Lastly, we notice that the GPT-3 model tends to generate responses that are substantially more verbose than $U3$, an observation that aligns with findings reported in several recent works (Goyal et al., 2023; Chiesurin et al., 2023).

These findings suggest that a significant reduction in the number of input tokens in these question-answer subconversations may not necessarily impact the generation of the follow-up response. This

	$U2_{long}$	$U2_{short}$	% condensing	$U3$	$U3_{long}$	$U3_{short}$
PD	10.44	3.673	64.8	17.98	86.37	86.24
CD	14.94	4.01	73.1	9.95	48.37	45.12
TD	17.44	4.60	73.5	12.81	55.13	50.19
TC	20.07	5.52	72.4	20.62	93.66	82.91
UD	15.15	3.83	74.7	9.68	113.20	124.31
Avg.	15.61	4.33	71.7	14.21	79.35	77.76

Table 4: Comparison of length differences of U_2 and U_3 across five datasets. Even though there's a substantial 64-75% compression from $U2_{long}$ to $U2_{short}$, the lengths of $U3_{long}$ to $U3_{short}$ remain consistently similar.

may be due to the presence of U_1 in the input which provides sufficient context for the model to generate the subsequent responses.

6 Conclusion

In this study, we explored the nuanced dynamics of utterance length in conversational modeling. Our investigation revealed that, particularly in question-answer and follow-up response contexts, significantly shorter utterances do not adversely impact the model's ability in generating coherent and contextually appropriate follow-up responses.

The findings of this study suggest a potential avenue for exploring utterance length as a factor in enhancing the efficiency of language models for conversational tasks from a novel perspective. By acknowledging the effectiveness of shorter inputs, future research can examine alternative token reduction techniques and the linguistic nuances of shortened inputs, aiming to optimize the balance between brevity and performance.

Limitations

This work has a few notable limitations. First, we measured the quality of the generated texts ($U3_{long/short}$) by comparing them to the original dialogue utterance (U_3) as reference that was present in the dataset. However, in open-ended text generation, there can be several acceptable references. While our evaluation method captures essential aspects of the conversation, it might not cover every nuance. Recent LLM-based evaluations like G-Eval (Liu et al., 2023) which employs chain-of-thoughts or MEEP (Ferron et al., 2023) which focuses on estimating dialogue engagingness could offer deeper insights into the quality of the generated responses. Additionally, the original average length of U_3 was found to be substantially shorter than the responses generated by the LLM, which could further impact the evaluation scores. It may be worth experimenting with setting GPT-3's maximum token limit closer to the average length of U_3. It is also worth mentioning that our empirical analysis focuses on utterances which are preceded by a question, therefore, making the response somewhat less unexpected. The effectiveness of this approach in conversations with sudden topic drifts or changes remains to be studied. We also acknowledge that compressing U_2 using GPT-3 may not be the most efficient approach and a heuristic method would be more ideal for this experiment considering the efficiency factor.

Furthermore, this study was conducted with GPT-3, and since then, there have been significant advancements in the field of large language models, including the release of GPT-4 and other open-source models. Future work could benefit from replicating and extending this experiment with these advanced models to compare the effectiveness and efficiency of dialogue generation and compression.

Ethics Statement

We acknowledge that in conversation datasets of natural language, potential toxic data instances may exist, which may further negatively propagate throughout the modeling process. During the compressing of $U2_{long}$, it is possible that some utterances may become ambiguous or assume unintentional modified meaning.

Acknowledgements

We would like to thank the anonymous reviewers and the members of the PortNLP group for their insightful feedback. This research was supported by the NSF under grant number SAI-P-2228783 and CRII:RI-2246174.

References

Rania Abdelghani, Yen-Hsiang Wang, Xingdi Yuan, Tong Wang, Pauline Lucas, Hélène Sauzéon, and Pierre-Yves Oudeyer. 2023. Gpt-3-driven pedagogical agents to train children's curious question-asking skills. *International Journal of Artificial Intelligence in Education*.

Katherine Abramski, Salvatore Citraro, Luigi Lombardi, Giulio Rossetti, and Massimo Stella. 2023. Cognitive network science reveals bias in gpt-3, gpt-3.5 turbo, and gpt-4 mirroring math anxiety in high-school students. *Big Data and Cognitive Computing*, 7(3).

Ellen Gurman Bard, Anne H Anderson, Catherine Sotillo, Matthew Aylett, Gwyneth Doherty-Sneddon, and Alison Newlands. 2000. Controlling the intelligibility of referring expressions in dialogue. *Journal of memory and language*, 42(1):1–22.

Allan Bell. 1984. Language style as audience design. *Language in society*, 13(2):145–204.

Tom Brown, Benjamin Mann, Nick Ryder, Melanie Subbiah, Jared D Kaplan, Prafulla Dhariwal, Arvind Neelakantan, Pranav Shyam, Girish Sastry, Amanda Askell, et al. 2020. Language models are few-shot learners. *Advances in neural information processing systems*, 33:1877–1901.

Lingjiao Chen, Matei Zaharia, and James Zou. 2023. Frugalgpt: How to use large language models while reducing cost and improving performance.

Sabrina Chiesurin, Dimitris Dimakopoulos, Marco Antonio Sobrevilla Cabezudo, Arash Eshghi, Ioannis Papaioannou, Verena Rieser, and Ioannis Konstas. 2023. The dangers of trusting stochastic parrots: Faithfulness and trust in open-domain conversational question answering.

Michael Denkowski and Alon Lavie. 2014. Meteor universal: Language specific translation evaluation for any target language. In *Proceedings of the ninth workshop on statistical machine translation*, pages 376–380.

Jacob Devlin, Ming-Wei Chang, Kenton Lee, and Kristina Toutanova. 2019. BERT: Pre-training of deep bidirectional transformers for language understanding. In *Proceedings of the 2019 Conference of the North American Chapter of the Association for Computational Linguistics: Human Language Technologies, Volume 1 (Long and Short Papers)*, pages 4171–4186, Minneapolis, Minnesota. Association for Computational Linguistics.

Amila Ferron, Amber Shore, Ekata Mitra, and Ameeta Agrawal. 2023. MEEP: Is this engaging? prompting large language models for dialogue evaluation in multilingual settings. In *Findings of the Association for Computational Linguistics: EMNLP 2023*, pages 2078–2100, Singapore. Association for Computational Linguistics.

Karthik Gopalakrishnan, Behnam Hedayatnia, Qinlang Chen, Anna Gottardi, Sanjeev Kwatra, Anu Venkatesh, Raefer Gabriel, and Dilek Hakkani-Tür. 2019. Topical-Chat: Towards Knowledge-Grounded Open-Domain Conversations. In *Proc. Interspeech 2019*, pages 1891–1895.

Tanya Goyal, Junyi Jessy Li, and Greg Durrett. 2023. News summarization and evaluation in the era of gpt-3.

Shumpei Inoue, Tsungwei Liu, Son Nguyen, and Minh-Tien Nguyen. 2022. Enhance incomplete utterance restoration by joint learning token extraction and text generation. In *Proceedings of the 2022 Conference of the North American Chapter of the Association for Computational Linguistics: Human Language Technologies*, pages 3149–3158, Seattle, United States. Association for Computational Linguistics.

Cassandra L Jacobs and Maryellen C MacDonald. 2023. A chimpanzee by any other name: The contributions of utterance context and information density on word choice. *Cognition*, 230:105265.

Huiqiang Jiang, Qianhui Wu, Xufang Luo, Dongsheng Li, Chin-Yew Lin, Yuqing Yang, and Lili Qiu. 2023. Longllmlingua: Accelerating and enhancing llms in long context scenarios via prompt compression.

Katikapalli Subramanyam Kalyan. 2023. A survey of gpt-3 family large language models including chatgpt and gpt-4.

Hyunwoo Kim, Youngjae Yu, Liwei Jiang, Ximing Lu, Daniel Khashabi, Gunhee Kim, Yejin Choi, and Maarten Sap. 2022. Prosocialdialog: A prosocial backbone for conversational agents. In *EMNLP*.

Harsh Kumar, Ilya Musabirov, Jiakai Shi, Adele Lauzon, Kwan Kiu Choy, Ofek Gross, Dana Kulzhabayeva, and Joseph Jay Williams. 2022. Exploring the design of prompts for applying gpt-3 based chatbots: A mental wellbeing case study on mechanical turk. *arXiv preprint arXiv:2209.11344*.

Chin-Yew Lin. 2004. Rouge: A package for automatic evaluation of summaries. In *Text summarization branches out*, pages 74–81.

Qian Liu, Bei Chen, Jian-Guang Lou, Bin Zhou, and Dongmei Zhang. 2020. Incomplete utterance rewriting as semantic segmentation. *arXiv preprint arXiv:2009.13166*.

Yang Liu, Dan Iter, Yichong Xu, Shuohang Wang, Ruochen Xu, and Chenguang Zhu. 2023. G-eval: Nlg evaluation using gpt-4 with better human alignment.

Ryan Lowe, Nissan Pow, Iulian Serban, and Joelle Pineau. 2015. The ubuntu dialogue corpus: A large dataset for research in unstructured multi-turn dialogue systems.

Omkar Patil, Lena Reed, Kevin K. Bowden, Juraj Juraska, Wen Cui, Vrindavan Harrison, Rishi Rajasekaran, Angela Ramirez, Cecilia Li, Eduardo Zamora, Phillip Lee, Jeshwanth Bheemanpally, Rohan Pandey, Adwait Ratnaparkhi, and Marilyn Walker. 2023. Athena 2.0: Discourse and user modeling in open domain dialogue.

Lianhui Qin, Aditya Gupta, Shyam Upadhyay, Luheng He, Yejin Choi, and Manaal Faruqui. 2021. TIMEDIAL: Temporal commonsense reasoning in dialog. In *Proceedings of the 59th Annual Meeting of the Association for Computational Linguistics and the 11th International Joint Conference on Natural Language Processing (Volume 1: Long Papers)*, pages 7066–7076, Online. Association for Computational Linguistics.

J Schulman, B Zoph, C Kim, J Hilton, J Menick, J Weng, JFC Uribe, L Fedus, L Metz, M Pokorny, et al. 2022. Chatgpt: Optimizing language models for dialogue.

Kurt Shuster, Jing Xu, Mojtaba Komeili, Da Ju, Eric Michael Smith, Stephen Roller, Megan Ung, Moya Chen, Kushal Arora, Joshua Lane, et al. 2022. Blenderbot 3: a deployed conversational agent that continually learns to responsibly engage. *arXiv preprint arXiv:2208.03188*.

Hui Su, Xiaoyu Shen, Rongzhi Zhang, Fei Sun, Pengwei Hu, Cheng Niu, and Jie Zhou. 2019. Improving multi-turn dialogue modelling with utterance rewriter. *arXiv preprint arXiv:1906.07004*.

Anaïs Tack and Chris Piech. 2022. The ai teacher test: Measuring the pedagogical ability of blender and gpt-3 in educational dialogues. *arXiv preprint arXiv:2205.07540*.

Caroline Tagg and Philip Seargeant. 2014. Audience design and language choice in the construction and maintenance of translocal communities on social network sites. In *The language of social media*, pages 161–185. Springer.

Romal Thoppilan, Daniel De Freitas, Jamie Hall, Noam Shazeer, Apoorv Kulshreshtha, Heng-Tze Cheng, Alicia Jin, Taylor Bos, Leslie Baker, Yu Du, et al. 2022. Lamda: Language models for dialog applications. *arXiv preprint arXiv:2201.08239*.

Lei Wang and Ee-Peng Lim. 2023. Zero-shot next-item recommendation using large pretrained language models. *arXiv preprint arXiv:2304.03153*.

Zihao Wang, Ali Ahmadvand, Jason Choi, Payam Karisani, and Eugene Agichtein. 2023. Ericson: An interactive open-domain conversational search agent. *arXiv preprint arXiv:2304.02233*.

Tianyi Zhang*, Varsha Kishore*, Felix Wu*, Kilian Q. Weinberger, and Yoav Artzi. 2020. Bertscore: Evaluating text generation with bert. In *International Conference on Learning Representations*.

Pei Zhou, Karthik Gopalakrishnan, Behnam Hedayatnia, Seokhwan Kim, Jay Pujara, Xiang Ren, Yang Liu, and Dilek Hakkani-Tur. 2021. Commonsense-focused dialogues for response generation: An empirical study. In *Proceedings of the 22nd Annual Meeting of the Special Interest Group on Discourse and Dialogue*, Singapore and Online. Association for Computational Linguistics.

Author Index

Association for Computational Linguistics
209 N. Eighth Street
Stroudsburg, Pennsylvania 18360

ISBN 978-1-7138-9462-9

9 781713 894629

CURRAN ASSOCIATES INC.
proceedings.com

Seventh SIGHAN Workshop on Chinese Language Processing 2013

Held at the 6th International Joint Conference on Natural Language Processing (IJCNLP 2013)

Nagoya, Japan
14-18 October 2013

ISBN: 978-1-62993-544-7